RADICAL EQUALITY

ANTITHETICAL RACE THEORY

THE
BEAUTIFUL
HUMAN
FAMILY

PRISCILLA DOREMUS

Printed/published by Seven Bears Publishing in the United States of America.

First printing 2023.

Seven Bears Publishing
Sugar Land, TX 77479
www.sevenbearspublishing.com

SEVEN BEARS
PUBLISHING

ACKNOWLEDGMENTS

A special thanks to

God, Dan, Meredith, Dylan, Barbara Kois,
Melinda Martin, Cindy Stewart, Lisa Jones, Pop,
and every member of my extended family
for always encouraging me to keep writing.

Thank you.

PROLOGUE

This book is based on a theory about race, an antithetical race theory or non-race theory, about human beings. It is this theory, rooted and grounded in biblical principles, that forms the foundation of each supposition and premise in *Radical Equality*.

The term *antithetical* means *in direct opposition* to something. You may wonder what the *something* is that this race theory stands in opposition to or against. It stands in opposition to any idea that we as a human race would be governed or controlled by each other's race in any way. To put it another way, it is the antithesis, or opposite, of the idea that we collectively as people would be so base as to allow the color of our skin, eyes, or the nation in which we began our lives to determine our worth, our value, or our destiny upon this earth and beyond.

Being bound by a philosophy based on appearance or nationality is a slap in the face of freedom. We need only glance at nature to see that our wonderful Creator made us all so beautifully different so that we would thrive and flourish in all of our great differences together.

In the following pages we will examine this radical notion of equality or Antithetical Race Theory, a brief history of the human race and nations, the things that divide us, the things uniting us, the conundrum of culture, and the dream of a united human family. We will also study how and why we have arrived at a place where we fail to experience equality, and we will explore how Antithetical Race Theory might be grasped here and now.

My hope for you as you read this book is that you would believe equality is something to be grasped, and that it is possible to unite people in the ultimate truth, hope, and love that are found in the triune God who created us all.

CONTENTS

CHAPTER 1

THE THEORY

"There is neither Jew nor Greek, there is
neither slave nor free, there is no male and
female, for you are all one in Christ Jesus."

—Galatians 3:28

Antithetical Race Theory has one overarching tenet, that
the beliefs of a people group unite or divide them, rather
than the color of their skin or their nation of origin. Further, it
is the demonstration of these convictions that proves the belief
system.

Convictions can either be positive or negative. In the
context of positive convictions, a group of people advances and
grows when united by truth and love. An example of this is
found in the local church joining together to provide food and
clothing to those in need. Just a few hundred people are often
able to provide enough supplies to meet the needs of thousands
of people, and this encourages others in the local community to
do the same.

In the context of negative convictions, a group of people
can be united in an effort to do harm. A small example of this
is in a gang organized to rob people, or a group of internet
hackers stealing personal information. A larger example is that
of the Nazi regime in Germany. Their clear focus and one of

their twenty-five platform causes was to segregate Jews from their Aryan society and strip them of all political, legal, and civil rights.[1]

Further, if those with negative convictions are allowed to continue unthwarted in their efforts, they will thrive and grow in their wrongful aims until they are eventually destroyed by others or bring destruction upon themselves by means of their own devices.

Antithetical Race Theory views adversity, oppression, and suffering as tragic experiences of a fallen society—but that once these experiences are overcome—serve to strengthen and bind people together in unity of purpose. It rejects the ideas of reparations, reverse discrimination, and race as a crutch—which encourage selfish ambition and discourage merit and effort—preferring rather to embrace the notions of gratitude, courage, and determination, which strengthen an entire group of people. It accepts the ideas of truth, grace, and love as more than concepts—they are embodied in the person of Jesus Christ, Son of God, in whose image we are all created and loved equally.

Antithetical Race Theory espouses a belief unrelated to race or national origin, but it is rather a place of obedience to God's commands, where in His sovereignty, He has commanded a blessing. In His kingdom there are followers of Jesus and non-followers. These two *races* are supported by Scripture, which refers to a *holy race* in 1 Peter 2:9 which says, "But you are not like that, for you are a chosen people. You are royal priests, a holy nation, God's very own possession. As a result, you can show others the goodness of God, for he called you out of the darkness into his wonderful light." And the second *race*, those *of the world*, "The world would love you as one of its own if you belonged to it, but you are no longer part of the world. I chose you to come out of the world, so it hates you" (John 15:19).

Antithetical Race Theory opposes the idea that the color of one's skin or country of origin could, should, or would be the determining factor in his or her destiny or any aspect of worth as a human being. A human being's value is found in the soul and the fact that he or she was created in the image of a Holy God. Jesus tells us in Scripture that it is this soul that is worth more than anything else in all the world.

> "And what do you benefit if you gain the whole world but lose your own soul? Is anything worth more than your soul?"
>
> —MATTHEW 16:26

Antithetical Race Theory disagrees with the idea that an individual or group of people cannot change or be changed in terms of behavior and beliefs. It has seen evidence to the contrary, as in the story of Nineveh, recorded in Jonah 3:2–10:

> Arise, go to Nineveh, that great city, and call out against it the message that I tell you." So Jonah arose and went to Nineveh, according to the word of the Lord. Now Nineveh was an exceedingly great city, three days' journey in breadth. Jonah began to go into the city, going a day's journey. And he called out, "Yet forty days, and Nineveh shall be overthrown!" And the people of Nineveh believed God. They called for a fast and put on sackcloth, from the greatest of them to the least of them. The

word reached the king of Nineveh, and he arose from his throne, removed his robe, covered himself with sackcloth, and sat in ashes. And he issued a proclamation and published through Nineveh, "By the decree of the king and his nobles: Let neither man nor beast, herd nor flock, taste anything. Let them not feed or drink water, but let man and beast be covered with sackcloth, and let them call out mightily to God. Let everyone turn from his evil way and from the violence that is in his hands. Who knows? God may turn and relent and turn from his fierce anger, so that we may not perish." When God saw what they did, how they turned from their evil way, God relented of the disaster that he had said he would do to them, and he did not do it.

Beliefs move people. Conviction brings change. Courage is a requirement for strength.

Antithetical Race Theory believes there is good and there is evil. It believes there is one triune God and Father of all, and it believes there is an adversary, the devil.

It supposes no fear in listening—really listening—to the thoughts, ideas, and perspectives of another—perhaps contrary to one's own—in order that both might learn something.

It believes God makes His blessing fall on *all* people. He loves *all* people. Those outside His kingdom are not *guaranteed* a blessing, but rather remain under sin's curse because they are slaves to sin and condemned to an eternal death. Those inside His kingdom are guaranteed a blessing. Deuteronomy 28:1 says it this way, "If you fully obey the Lord your God and carefully keep all his commands that I am giving you today, the Lord your God will set you high above all the nations of the world." This blessing is God's command for them. They are redeemed from sin's curse. They are slaves to Jesus, which makes them truly free in every sense of the word, regardless of circumstance, as this freedom is a condition of the heart. The commanded blessing does not mean that everything in life will go well for them, but rather the commanded blessing extends beyond earthly life into eternity and is, therefore, contingent upon an eternal timeline.

Blessed does not mean *better than* or *superior to*, lest we follow the path of the Pharisees of old. *Blessed* does not mean any group or ideology placing itself above another. Blessed simply means *blessed*. Antithetical Race Theory requires humility.

Antithetical Race Theory believes love for God must surpass love of country.

This is Antithetical Race Theory.

CHAPTER 2

THE HUMAN RACE AND NATIONS

"But you are a chosen race, a royal priesthood,
a holy nation, a people for his own possession,
that you may proclaim the excellencies of him
who called you out of darkness into his marvelous light."

—1 Peter 2:9

In order to examine the human race and further understand from what place Antithetical Race Theory is derived, we must first ask the question, Where did the human race and nations have their beginning?

Starting with the Book of Genesis in the Holy Bible, we learn that Adam and Eve, parents of all living people, are not described in terms of race or skin color at all. They are described in terms of their gender.

"So God created man in his own image,
in the image of God he created him;
male and female he created them."

—Genesis 1:27

The two genders were blessed to have different roles and were gifted in specific ways in which to carry out these roles. One role was not lesser than the other, simply different. Just as the hand is not lesser than the foot, each gender was simply designed differently for its specific role in blessing the body. And so it is with people.

The color of one's skin, while there is a beautiful nuance about them, was less important in the grander scheme, and we find very little mention of it at all in early historical writings, suggesting it was more intended as the color on a flower or the variety of color in the feathers of a bird—drawing you into their beauty and spectacular difference. So we are drawn into the beauty and magnificent differences in one another.

But these beautiful differences soon spiraled into evil intentions. The Holy Bible gives us the result:

> The Lord saw that the wickedness of man was great in the earth, and that every intention of the thoughts of his heart was only evil continually. And the Lord regretted that he had made man on the earth, and it grieved him to his heart. So the Lord said, "I will blot out man whom I have created from the face of the land, man and animals and creeping things and birds of the heavens, for I am sorry that I have made them." But Noah found favor in the eyes of the Lord. These are the generations of Noah. Noah was a righteous man, blameless in his generation. Noah walked with God.
>
> —GENESIS 6:5–10

As the human race begins again after the great flood with the family of Noah, we find the nations beginning to emerge and take shape. The people who left the ark were eight in number: Noah, his wife, their three sons, Shem, Ham, Japheth, and the wife of each of the three sons. Genesis 9:18–19 tells us: "The sons of Noah who went forth from the ark were Shem, Ham, and Japheth. [Ham was the father of Canaan.] These three were the sons of Noah, and from these the people of the whole earth were dispersed."

From these we know that Shem begat the Israeli, Asian, and Arab nations. Ham's offspring became the nation of Canaan and spread into the continent of Africa. Canaan, Ham's son, was cursed to be the servant of Shem and Japheth. This happened because Ham looked at his father, Noah, while he was naked and drunk in his tent and then told his two brothers (Genesis 9). Japheth is considered the father of the Turkish, Slavic, and European nations.

The human race was further dispersed in the land of Shinar when the people, united in both language and intention, began to erect a tower to the heavens, commonly referred to as the Tower of Babel.

> Now the whole earth had one language and the same words. And as people migrated from the east, they found a plain in the land of Shinar and settled there. And they said to one another, "Come, let us make bricks, and burn them thoroughly." And they had brick for stone, and bitumen for mortar. Then they said, "Come, let us build ourselves a city and a tower with its top in the heavens, and let us make a name for ourselves, lest we be dispersed over the face of the whole earth." And the Lord came down to see the city and the tower, which the children of man had built. And the Lord said,

"Behold, they are one people, and they have all one language, and this is only the beginning of what they will do. And nothing that they propose to do will now be impossible for them. Come, let us go down and there confuse their language, so that they may not understand one another's speech. So the Lord dispersed them from there over the face of all the earth, and they left off building the city. Therefore its name was called Babel, because there the Lord confused the language of all the earth. And from there the Lord dispersed them over the face of all the earth."

—GENESIS 11:1–9

While it is often wondered why God did not want the people united in this quest, it was their shared conviction to make a name for themselves rather than God that united them in building this great tower. We were created to worship God and love our neighbor. Clearly things that God did not see in this pursuit.

In light of this dispersion, we note and can reasonably assume that the division of Shem, Ham, and Japheth's descendants was not an exact science with regard to the nations previously attributed to them, but that there was undoubtedly some overlap with families, people groups, and tribes joining with others and intermarrying. This is confirmed throughout history in recorded genealogies dating back thousands of years.[2]

After this, in Genesis chapters 11 through 25 we learn about a man named Abram whom God called to follow Him. Abram had no idea where God was leading him, but he had the faith to go and finally settled in a place called Hebron in the land of Canaan. God made a covenant of circumcision with Abram and changed his name to Abraham.

> When Abram was ninety-nine years old the Lord appeared to Abram and said to him, "I am God Almighty; walk before me, and be blameless, that I may make my covenant between me and you, and may multiply you greatly." Then Abram fell on his face. And God said to him, "Behold, my covenant is with you, and you shall be the father of a multitude of nations. No longer shall your name be called Abram, but your name shall be Abraham, for I have made you the father of a multitude of nations. I will make you exceedingly fruitful, and I will make you into nations, and kings shall come from you. And I will establish my covenant between me and you and your off-spring after you throughout their generations for an everlasting covenant, to be God to you and to your offspring after you. And I will give to you and to your offspring after you the land of your sojournings, all the land of Canaan, for an everlasting possession, and I will be their God."
>
> And God said to Abraham, "As for you, you shall keep my covenant, you and your offspring after you throughout their generations. This is

my covenant, which you shall keep, between
me and you and your offspring after you:
Every male among you shall be circumcised.
You shall be circumcised in the flesh of your
foreskins, and it shall be a sign of the covenant
between me and you. He who is eight days old
among you shall be circumcised. Every male
throughout your generations, whether born in
your house or bought with your money from
any foreigner who is not of your offspring,
both he who is born in your house and he who
is bought with your money, shall surely be
circumcised. So shall my covenant be in your
flesh an everlasting covenant. Any uncircum-
cised male who is not circumcised in the flesh
of his foreskin shall be cut off from his people;
he has broken my covenant."

—Genesis 17:1–14

God also blessed Sarai, Abraham's wife, changing her name
to Sarah and promising a son through her who would be the
son of God's covenant with Abraham.

And God said to Abraham, "As for Sarai your
wife, you shall not call her name Sarai, but
Sarah shall be her name. I will bless her, and
moreover, I will give you a son by her. I will
bless her, and she shall become nations; kings
of peoples shall come from her." Then Abraham fell on his face and laughed and said to
himself, "Shall a child be born to a man who is

a hundred years old? Shall Sarah, who is ninety years old, bear a child?" And Abraham said to God, "Oh that Ishmael might live before you!" God said, "No, but Sarah your wife shall bear you a son, and you shall call his name Isaac. I will establish my covenant with him as an everlasting covenant for his offspring after him. As for Ishmael, I have heard you; behold, I have blessed him and will make him fruitful and multiply him greatly. He shall father twelve *princes, and I will make him into a great nation. But I will establish my covenant with Isaac, whom Sarah shall bear to you at this time next year."*

—GENESIS 17:15–21, EMPHASIS ADDED.

Abraham is considered to be the father of two large nations of people in history. His son, Isaac, renamed Israel, is deemed the father of the Jews, the Israeli people. His son, Ishmael, whose mother was Hagar, Sarah's Egyptian maidservant, became the father of the twelve Arabian princes. God promised Abraham the land of Canaan, all the land from the River of Egypt to the Euphrates River, for his son Isaac.

Notice in Genesis 25 how Abraham scattered the rest of his own sons, separating them geographically to the east, away from Isaac, the son of the promise.

Abraham took another wife, whose name was Keturah. She bore him Zimran, Jokshan, Medan, Midian, Ishbak, and Shuah. Jokshan fathered Sheba and Dedan. The sons of Dedan

were Asshurim, Letushim, and Leummim. The
sons of Midian were Ephah, Epher, Hanoch,
Abida, and Eldaah. All these were the children
of Keturah. Abraham gave all he had to Isaac.
But to the sons of his concubines Abraham
gave gifts, and while he was still living he sent
them away from his son Isaac, eastward to the
east country.

—Genesis 25:1–6

This is significant because God's promised blessing to Abraham for having faith enough to follow Him was to come from
the family line of the one son, Isaac. This was the son whom
God promised to Abraham.

We learn further that Ishmael's sons settled in the rich
country east of Egypt.

This is the account of the family of Ishmael, the
son of Abraham through Hagar, Sarah's Egyptian servant. Here is a list, by their names and
clans, of Ishmael's descendants: The oldest was
Nebaioth, followed by Kedar, Adbeel, Mibsam,
Mishma, Dumah, Massa, Hadad, Tema, Jetur,
Naphish, and Kedemah. These twelve sons
of Ishmael became the founders of twelve
tribes named after them, listed according to
the places they settled and camped. Ishmael
lived for 137 years. Then he breathed his last
and joined his ancestors in death. Ishmael's
descendants occupied the region from Havilah
to Shur, which is east of Egypt in the direction

of Asshur. There they lived in open hostility
toward all their relatives.

—GENESIS 25:12–18

And the fighting has continued ever since.

But it was the faith of Abraham that gained favor in the eyes
of God rather than the color of Abraham's skin, his national
origin, or that he was a descendant of Shem.

> "So the promise is received by faith. It is given
> as a free gift. And we are all certain to receive it
> if we have faith like Abraham's. For Abraham
> is the father of all who believe."

—ROMANS 4:16

We see in this passage of Scripture that the promise was not
exclusive or kept for Abraham's descendants alone. Under the
New Covenant through Jesus Christ, this promised blessing was
available to all mankind.

But even the Israelites endured slavery and persecution
because of their race. This often happens in nations and cultures in which one group is elevated above another. The Holy
Bible tells us about this time for the Jews. When Jacob's son,
Joseph, became second in command to Pharaoh for all of Egypt,
a severe famine occurred such that the surrounding nations
came to Egypt to buy grain. It was during this time that Joseph
invited his father, brother, and all their families to live in Egypt
and tend their flocks and herds—something detestable to the
Egyptians. As the Israelites grew in strength and number and
a new Pharaoh who knew nothing about Joseph rose to power,
fear took hold of this new Pharaoh and the Egyptian people,
fear that the Jews could easily overpower them.

Exodus 1:8–14 gives the account:

> Now there arose a new king over Egypt, who
> did not know Joseph. And he said to his
> people, "Behold, the people of Israel are too
> many and too mighty for us. Come, let us
> deal shrewdly with them, lest they multiply,
> and, if war breaks out, they join our enemies
> and fight against us and escape from the land."
> Therefore they set taskmasters over them to
> afflict them with heavy burdens. They built for
> Pharaoh store cities, Pithom and Raamses. But
> the more they were oppressed, the more they
> multiplied and the more they spread abroad.
> And the Egyptians were in dread of the people
> of Israel. So they ruthlessly made the people of
> Israel work as slaves and made their lives bitter
> with hard service, in mortar and brick, and in
> all kinds of work in the field. In all their work
> they ruthlessly made them work as slaves.

In the 2,666th year after creation, God heard the cries
of the Jewish people held captive and cruelly enslaved in
Egypt and sent them a deliverer in the humblest of men,
Moses (Numbers 12:3). Yet in spite of this deliverance, the
Israelites failed to have any true belief system. Many followed
God for what they could get from Him and tended to quickly
fall away. Most of the people had no real change of heart.

During the Babylonian exile from roughly 608 BC to 538
BC, we see more of the same behavior of the Israelites toward

God and learn that God preserved a remnant of the nation of Israel during the period of their captivity by the Babylonians.

In the many battles both before and after this time period, we find the intermarrying and intermixing of the nations and different cultures, much like we see today, though God warned the Israeli people not to intermarry lest they be led astray from Him and follow other gods.

> "When the Lord your God hands these nations over to you and you conquer them, you must completely destroy them. Make no treaties with them and show them no mercy. You must not intermarry with them. Do not let your daughters and sons marry their sons and daughters, for they will lead your children away from me to worship other gods. Then the anger of the Lord will burn against you, and he will quickly destroy you."
>
> —DEUTERONOMY 7:24

While some view this command not to intermarry as exclusive or twist the passage of Scripture to mean something other than simply the protection of a group of people, it further reinforces the Antithetical Race Theory, as it is in the commonality of beliefs—this place of faith in the triune God which is open to all mankind—that He commands His blessing. When God commands the people not to intermarry, He tells them why. He says, "They will lead your children away from me to worship other gods." When the people disobeyed God in this way, that is exactly what happened. This is evidenced repeatedly throughout Scripture.

In the book of Judges, we see yet another example of the Israelites turning their backs on God and coming out from under their commanded place of blessing:

> And the people of Israel did what was evil in the sight of the Lord and served the Baals. And they abandoned the Lord, the God of their fathers, who had brought them out of the land of Egypt. They went after other gods, from among the gods of the peoples who were around them, and bowed down to them. And they provoked the Lord to anger. They abandoned the Lord and served the Baals and the Ashtaroth. So the anger of the Lord was kindled against Israel, and he gave them over to plunderers, who plundered them. And he sold them into the hand of their surrounding enemies, so that they could no longer withstand their enemies. Whenever they marched out, the hand of the Lord was against them for harm, as the Lord had warned, and as the Lord had sworn to them. And they were in terrible distress.
>
> —JUDGES 2:11–15

While 1 Peter 2:9 was written to Jewish Christians, it was and is God's design that all people would be believers in the triune God and all would follow Him in becoming what Scripture calls *true Jews* (Romans 2:29), thereby becoming a part of a chosen race, a royal priesthood, a holy nation, a people for his own possession—not to be better than or to lord it over anyone—but quite the opposite. God's people were and are today to be the servants of all, to humbly and gratefully proclaim the excellencies of Him who called all people out of darkness into the His marvelous light—the Creator Himself. But not all people would choose this way.

Let us examine the more recent reality of this belief as it has played out in the nations of the world over the past few hundred years.

The European Reformation (1517–1600) ushered in an afront to the manner in which church had socially, culturally, and historically been constructed and conducted in western Europe. It ended in the creation of what is considered the global Protestant Church of today. It was the courage of one man, Martin Luther, posting his *Ninety-Five Theses on the Power and Efficacy of Indulgences* to the Archbishop of Mainz on the door of the church in Wittenberg, Saxony-Anhalt, Germany, on October 31, 1517, that brought about sweeping change. Luther's chief complaints included the idea of purgatory and that the Catholic church allowed parishioners to quite literally purchase the right to sin by buying something called indulgences. He also believed that the Bible is the sole infallible source of authority for Christian faith and practice (the doctrine called sola scriptura).

Luther was excommunicated from the Catholic Church in 1521, and later in his life wrote what were considered to be a number of quite controversial anti-Semitic teachings, condemning Judaism for its practices, which he believed to be in complete opposition to Christianity. This was due in large part to his failure in converting European Jews to Christianity.

Consider that for a moment—a long moment.

It is a dangerous thing to portray an entire nation or race of people in a certain light, whether positive or negative, based on the beliefs of a subpopulation.

In the history and formation of the United States of America, we can read in the Mayflower Compact the purpose and reason the settlers came to the New World. They were a motley crew to be sure, made up of Puritan Separatists, men and women seeking something different from the status quo, and others hoping to ply their trade with a new and growing opportunity.

Yet they were united by their conviction to glorify God and advance the Christian faith, so much so that it became the basis of this document, originally called the *Agreement Between the Settlers of New Plymouth*, lest there be any doubt as to why they had come. The original *Mayflower Compact* text reads as follows:

> In the name of God, Amen. We, whose names are underwritten, the loyal subjects of our dread Sovereigne Lord, King James, by the grace of God, of Great Britaine, France and Ireland king, defender of the faith, etc. having undertaken, for the glory of God, and advancement of the Christian faith, and honour of our king and country, a voyage to plant the first colony in the Northerne parts of Virginia, doe by these presents solemnly and mutually in the presence of God and one of another, covenant and combine ourselves together into a civill body politick, for our better ordering and preservation, and furtherance of the ends aforesaid; and by virtue hereof to enacte, constitute, and frame such just and equall laws, ordinances, acts, constitutions and

offices, from time to time, as shall be thought most meete and convenient for the generall good of the Colonie unto which we promise all due submission and obedience. In witness whereof we have hereunder subscribed our names at Cape-Codd the 11. of November, in the year of the raigne of our sovereigne lord, King James, of England, France and Ireland, the eighteenth, and of Scotland the fiftie-fourth. Anno Dom. 1620.[3]

While the passengers of the Mayflower and settlers of Plymouth Colony were most certainly united in their purpose at the time of writing, we find it didn't take long for the sheep to wander off course. The Mayflower Compact was repealed sixty-six years later in 1686, reinstated in 1689, and repealed again in 1691, not much different from what we find happening in America and other countries today, or that we read about in Old Testament history with the nation of Israel and the early New Testament followers of *The Way*.

The Age of Enlightenment (1688–1815) brought the idea that human reasoning was the ticket to answering all of life's questions. The movement debuted after the English Civil Wars and is considered to have ended with the Napoleonic Wars. The ideas of religious tolerance, pride of the individual, and many advances in science and politics—which were in complete contrast to the historical constructs—were all earmarks of this era. There were many with emerging and different thoughts during this time, including John Wilkes, a radical journalist who sought to remove God from anything and everything he touched, and John Locke (*Two Treatises of Government*, 1689). These and many others were credited with bringing about much of the cultural and political reforms during the time period, which included a powerful rise in industrialism and the wealth of the common man.

The First Great Awakening (1730–1760)[4] was a time of revival and increased spiritual conviction and enthusiasm in following the teachings of Jesus and repenting of sin. It began in America among already practicing Christians and the Bible teaching of a British itinerant preacher named George Whitefield. Whitefield's teaching was supported by British, German, and Dutch immigrants to America, as well as numerous Protestant denominations. While Whitefield's teaching of the Holy Bible—rather than following the ways of tradition—was busy turning the New World upside down, this shared belief also had a strong impact on democratic thought and practice in America, uniting colonists and statesmen in creating the legal and political framework currently under siege in America.

Not long after this time, back in England, William Wilberforce, a wealthy British politician and Christian, was fighting long and hard to abolish the slave trade in Europe. This long political battle culminated in the passage of the Slave Trade Act of 1807. Wilberforce believed strongly in the equality of all people and succeeded in upending the greed that was devoid of morality that brought the trade of human beings into practice to begin with. His was not an easy task, but it was a worthy and courageous one that still pays dividends today and would continue its positive spread to nations around the world.

One of those nations was the United States of America. In this country, it was the American Civil War (1861–1865)[5] pitting the North against the South for the abolition of slavery. The North believed slavery was a moral wrong, while the South was deeply entrenched in the slave trade and the personal gain derived from it. The war was a bloodbath in which approximately 620,000 people lost their lives. And much like Wilberforce's tireless efforts in Europe, it was the belief system of one man, Abraham Lincoln, which made all the difference. On January 1, 1863, the *Emancipation Proclamation* was signed into law, freeing the slaves who had been brought to America primarily from the continent of Africa. The transcript of the Proclamation was quite telling:

By the President of the United States of America:

A Proclamation.

Whereas, on the twenty-second day of September, in the year of our Lord one thousand eight hundred and sixty-two, a proclamation was issued by the President of the United States, containing, among other things, the following, to wit:

That on the first day of January, in the year of our Lord one thousand eight hundred and sixty-three, all persons held as slaves within any State or designated part of a State, the people whereof shall then be in rebellion against the United States, shall be then, thenceforward, and forever free; and the Executive Government of the United States, including the military and naval authority thereof, will recognize and maintain the freedom of such persons, and will do no act or acts to repress such persons, or any of them, in any efforts they may make for their actual freedom.

That the Executive will, on the first day of January aforesaid, by proclamation, designate the States and parts of

States, if any, in which the people thereof, respectively, shall then be in rebellion against the United States; and the fact that any State, or the people thereof, shall on that day be, in good faith, represented in the Congress of the United States by members chosen thereto at elections wherein a majority of the qualified voters of such State shall have participated, shall, in the absence of strong countervailing testimony, be deemed conclusive evidence that such State, and the people thereof, are not then in rebellion against the United States.

Now, therefore I, Abraham Lincoln, President of the United States, by virtue of the power in me vested as Commander-in-Chief, of the Army and Navy of the United States in time of actual armed rebellion against the authority and government of the United States, and as a fit and necessary war measure for suppressing said rebellion, do, on this first day of January, in the year of our Lord one thousand eight hundred and sixty-three, and in accordance with my purpose so to do publicly proclaimed for the full period of one hundred days, from the day first above mentioned, order and designate as the States and parts of States wherein the people thereof respectively, are this day in rebellion against the United States, the following, to wit:

Arkansas, Texas, Louisiana, (except the Parishes of St. Bernard, Plaquemines, Jefferson, St. John, St. Charles, St. James Ascension, Assumption, Terrebonne, Lafourche, St. Mary, St. Martin, and Orleans, including the City of New Orleans) Mississippi, Alabama,

Florida, Georgia, South Carolina, North Carolina, and Virginia, (except the forty-eight counties designated as West Virginia, and also the counties of Berkley, Accomac, Northampton, Elizabeth City, York, Princess Ann, and Norfolk, including the cities of Norfolk and Portsmouth), and which excepted parts, are for the present, left precisely as if this proclamation were not issued.

And by virtue of the power, and for the purpose aforesaid, I do order and declare that all persons held as slaves within said designated States, and parts of States, are, and henceforward shall be free; and that the Executive government of the United States, including the military and naval authorities thereof, will recognize and maintain the freedom of said persons.

And I hereby enjoin upon the people so declared to be free to abstain from all violence, unless in necessary self-defence; and I recommend to them that, in all cases when allowed, they labor faithfully for reasonable wages.

And I further declare and make known, that such persons of suitable condition, will be received into the armed service of the United States to garrison forts, positions, stations, and other places, and to man vessels of all sorts in said service.

And upon this act, sincerely believed to be an act of justice, warranted by the Constitution, upon military necessity, I invoke the considerate judgment of mankind, and the gracious favor of Almighty God.

In witness whereof, I have hereunto set my hand and caused the seal of the United States to be affixed.

Done at the City of Washington, this first day of January, in the year of our Lord one thousand eight hundred and sixty-three, and of the Independence of the United States of America the eighty-seventh.

By the President:

ABRAHAM LINCOLN

WILLIAM H. SEWARD, Secretary of State.[6]

World War I (1914–1919)[7] was arguably one of the two most notable examples of negative conviction in Antithetical Race Theory. The other being World War II. It was in the late 1800s when Germany's unified Reich and strength from its rapid growth and industrial expansion began to covet the power of the British Royal Navy, longing to dominate and surpass its power. Russia was still licking its wounds from defeats in the Russo-Japanese War and subsequent Russian Revolution of 1905. Austria annexed Bosnia and Herzegovina of the failing Ottoman Empire, whose new capital city became Sarajevo. These and many, many more disruptive events underpinned by governments bent on dominance, as their belief system, left the people in these nations vulnerable in every way.

Without stable leadership and a positive unified vision, these fragile nations found themselves hair-trigger-ready for conflict, and on June 28, 1914, when Archduke Franz Ferdinand of Austria was assassinated by a group of six men hoping to free Bosnia from Austrian rule, the trigger was pulled.

The conflict was so wide-sweeping and with such splintered interests that by the time the conflict was ending, most forgot why and for what they had even begun to fight, but knowing now just exactly what they wanted—mainly peace. And so, the conflict was formally ended on June 28, 1919, with the Treaty of Versailles, five years to the day after the assassination of Archduke Ferdinand.

But there were issues that remained unresolved.

Germany was held responsible for World War I in the Treaty of Versailles and required to pay reparations. Part of the German reparations to Japan resulted in Germany giving up land they held in China to the Japanese. While Japan found this a suitable result of the war, China did not. As a result, Chinese bitterness toward the West continued to fester and grow, leaving China weak and exposed, distracting it from what really mattered—its own belief system. But China was not the only country in this position.

Twenty years later, we find World War II (1939–1945)[8] beginning when Adolf Hitler invaded Poland on September 1, 1939. This was a fascist act, as fascism promotes ultimate superlative military strength, and the supremacy of one nation and its leader to the detriment of its citizens and the countries around it. The fascist belief system originated with Benito Mussolini, Prime Minister and dictator of Italy, and spread rapidly through the vulnerable nations—all greedy for power and real estate. The dehumanizing and hideous destruction of the Jews was a major outgrowth of fascism. The radical Antifa terrorists today mis-define fascism to excuse their terrorism on the population. Sadly, the philosophical and political construct is still alive and well today.

The Allied nations, the Soviet Union, United Kingdom, China, the United States of America, and a number of smaller nations joined together to defeat Germany. But it was only after significant changes in power that peace was finally achieved. On April 12, 1945, President Roosevelt died and was replaced by his Vice President, Harry Truman. On April 28, 1945, Benito Mussolini was killed and succeeded by Pietro Badoglio. And it was on April 30, 1945, that Hitler committed suicide and was followed by Karl Donitz. Just one week later, on May 7, 1945, the Germans signed the Unconditional Surrender of the Wehrmacht, thus ending the bulk of the war.

But World War II's evil toll on human lives was just beginning to unfold. Most notable was the discovery of Nazi concentration camps and extermination camps, killing an estimated six million Jews, nearly three million Poles, four million disabled or people considered unfit for life.[9] It was and is an unthinkable evil.

Regrettably, this was just a prelude to what was soon to be exposed as at least fifteen million people were tortured and killed in the Soviet Gulag labor camps, through mass murder, famine, and other unthinkable tortures under Joseph Stalin from 1924 to 1953.[10]

In the aftermath of these events and on the heels of the Vietnam and Korean Wars, a generation of young Americans was in search of something different. They wanted change but weren't sure just where to find that change. They sought it in drugs, alcohol, rebelling against the establishment, and finally found that real transformation takes place in a personal relationship with Jesus Christ. The movement was coined the Jesus Movement or Jesus Revolution (roughly, 1950–2000).[11]

One of the most prominent figures during this movement was a young dairy farmer's son named Billy Graham. Graham was called by God to become an evangelist and he preached sermons telling of the Good News, that a belief in the triune God brings about massive change in a person's heart and life. The searching youth and hippies[12] of the time finally had their answer. It is estimated that 2.2 million people chose this life change as a result of Billy Graham's ministry.[13]

In discussing these historical events, I would be remiss not to mention the antithesis of Antithetical Race Theory. It is the single greatest enemy to the human being in terms of social and political constructs, and it is the likes of communism, fascism, Marxism, and socialism—whose ideologies are proven enemies of the people. It is the spread of these evils, their oppressive and constrictive nature, and their devaluation of the human soul, that the free world must oppose with all of its might.

In order to better understand why these constructs are evil and the familiar pattern giving rise to them, let us examine a few of them in greater detail.

We need only talk to individuals living in these countries before their fall to communism, socialism, fascism, and Marxism, to have a clear picture of the change. One very specific example of this was written by Kitty Werthmann:

> What I am about to tell you is something you've probably never heard or will ever read in history books. I believe that I am an eyewitness to history. I cannot tell you that Hitler took Austria by tanks and guns; it would distort history. We elected him by a landslide – 98% of the vote. I've never read that in any American

publications. Everyone thinks that Hitler just rolled in with his tanks and took Austria by force.

In 1938, Austria was in a deep depression. Nearly one-third of our workforce was unemployed. We had 25% inflation and 25% bank loan interest rates. Farmers and businesspeople were declaring bankruptcy daily. Young people were going from house to house begging for food. Not that they didn't want to work. There simply weren't any jobs. My mother was a Christian woman and believed in helping the needy. Every day we cooked a big kettle of soup and baked bread to feed those poor, hungry people--about 30 daily.

The Communist Party and the National Socialist Party were fighting each other. Blocks and blocks of cities like Vienna, Linz, and Graz were destroyed. The people became desperate and petitioned the government to let them decide what kind of government they wanted.

We looked to our neighbor on the north, Germany, where Hitler had been in power since 1933. We had been told that they didn't have unemployment or crime, and they had a high standard of living. Nothing was ever said about persecution of any group--Jewish or otherwise. We were led to believe that everyone was happy. We wanted the same way of life in Austria. We were promised that a vote for Hitler would mean the end of unemployment and help for the family. Hitler also said that businesses would be assisted, and farmers would get their farms back. Ninety-eight percent of the population voted to annex Austria to Germany and have Hitler for our ruler. We were overjoyed, and for three days we danced in the streets and had candlelight parades. The new government opened big field kitchens, and everyone was fed.

After the election, German officials were appointed, and like a miracle, we suddenly had law and order. Three or four weeks later, everyone was employed. The government made sure that a lot of work was created through the Public Work Service. Hitler decided we should have equal rights for women. Before this, it was a custom that married Austrian women did not work outside the home. An able-bodied husband would be looked down on if he couldn't support his family. Many women in the teaching profession were elated that they could retain the jobs they previously had been required to give up for marriage.

Hitler Targets Education – Eliminates Religious Instruction for Children

Our education was nationalized. I attended a very good public school. The population was predominantly Catholic, so we had religion in our schools. The day we elected Hitler (March 13, 1938), I walked into my schoolroom to find the crucifix replaced by Hitler's picture hanging next to a Nazi flag. Our teacher, a very devout woman, stood up and told the class we wouldn't pray or have religion anymore. Instead, we sang "Deutschland, Deutschland, Uber Alles," and had physical education.

Sunday became National Youth Day with compulsory attendance. Parents were not pleased about the sudden change in curriculum. They were told that if they did not send us, they would receive a stiff letter of warning the first time. The second time they would be fined the equivalent of $300, and the third time they would be subject to jail. The first two hours consisted of political indoctrination. The rest of the day we had sports. As time went along, we loved it. Oh, we had so much fun and got our sports equipment free. We would go home and gleefully tell our parents about the wonderful time we had.

My mother was very unhappy. When the next term started, she took me out of public school and put me in a convent. I told her she couldn't do that, and she told me that someday when I grew up, I would be grateful. There was a very good curriculum, but hardly any fun--no sports, and no political indoctrination. I hated it at first but felt I could tolerate it.

Every once in a while, on holidays, I went home. I would go back to my old friends and ask what was going on and what they were doing. Their loose lifestyle was very alarming to me. They lived without religion. By that time unwed mothers were glorified for having a baby for Hitler. It seemed strange to me that our society had changed so suddenly. As time went along, I realized what a great deed my Mother did so that I wasn't exposed to that kind of humanistic philosophy.

Equal Rights Hits Home

In 1939, the war started, and a food bank was established. All food was rationed and could only be purchased using food stamps. At the same time, a full-employment law was passed which meant if you didn't work, you didn't get a ration card, and if you didn't have a card, you starved to death. Women who stayed home to raise their families didn't have any marketable skills and often had to take jobs more suited for men. Soon after this, the draft was implemented. It was compulsory for young people, male and female, to give one year to the labor corps. During the day, the girls worked on the farms, and at night they returned to their barracks for military training just like the boys. They were trained to be anti-aircraft gunners and participated in the signal corps. After the labor corps, they were not discharged but were used in the front lines. When I go back to Austria to visit my family and friends, most of these women are emotional cripples because they just were not equipped to handle the horrors of combat. Three months before I turned 18, I was severely injured in an air raid attack. I nearly had a leg amputated, so I was spared having to go into the labor corps and into military service.

Hitler Restructured the Family Through Daycare

When the mothers had to go out into the workforce, the government immediately established child care centers. You could take your children ages 4 weeks to school age and leave them there around-the-clock, 7 days a week, under the total care of the government. The state raised a whole generation of children. There were no motherly women to take care of the children—just people highly trained in child psychology. By this time, no one talked about equal rights. We knew we had been had.

Before Hitler, we had very good medical care. Many American doctors trained at the University of Vienna. After Hitler, health care was socialized, free for everyone. Doctors were salaried by the government. The problem was, since it was free, the people were going to the doctors for everything. When the good doctor arrived at his office at 8 a.m., 40 people were already waiting and, at the same time, the hospitals were full. If you needed elective surgery, you had to wait a year or two for your turn. There was no money for research as it was poured into socialized medicine. Research at the medical schools literally stopped, so the best doctors left Austria and emigrated to other countries.

As for health care, our tax rates went up to 80% of our income. Newlyweds immediately received a $1,000 loan from the government to establish a household. We had big programs for families. All day care and education were free. High schools were taken over by the government and college tuition was subsidized. Everyone was entitled to free handouts, such as food stamps, clothing, and housing. We had another agency designed to monitor business. My brother-in-law owned a restaurant that had square tables. Government officials told him he had to replace them with round tables because people might bump themselves on the corners. Then they said he had to have additional bathroom facilities. It was just a small dairy business with a snack bar. He couldn't meet all the demands. Soon, he went out of business. If the government owned the large businesses and not many small ones existed, it could be in control.

We had consumer protection. We were told how to shop and what to buy. Free enterprise was essentially abolished. We had a planning agency specially designed for farmers. The agents would go to the farms, count the livestock, then tell the farmers what to produce, and how to produce it.

"Mercy Killing" Redefined

In 1944, I was a student teacher in a small village in the Alps. The villagers were surrounded by mountain passes which, in the winter, were closed off with snow, causing people to be isolated. So people intermarried and offspring were sometimes retarded. When I arrived, I was told there were 15 mentally retarded adults but they were all useful and did good manual work. I knew one, named Vincent, very well. He was a janitor of the school. One day I looked out the window and saw Vincent and others getting into a van. I asked my superior where they were going. She said to an institution where the State Health Department would teach them a trade, and to read and write. The families were required to sign papers with a little clause that they could not visit for 6 months. They were told visits would interfere with the program and might cause homesickness.

As time passed, letters started to dribble back saying these people died a natural, merciful death. The villagers were not fooled. We suspected what was happening.

Those people left in excellent physical health and all died within 6 months. We called this *euthanasia*.

The Final Steps—Gun Laws

Next came gun registration. People were getting injured by guns. Hitler said that the real way to catch criminals (we still had a few) was by matching serial numbers on guns. Most citizens were law abiding and dutifully marched to the police station to register their firearms. Not long afterwards, the police said that it was best for everyone to turn in their guns. The authorities already knew who had them, so it was futile not to comply voluntarily. No more freedom of speech. Anyone who said something against the government was taken away. We knew many people who were arrested, not only Jews, but also priests and ministers who spoke up.

Totalitarianism didn't come quickly, it took 5 years from 1938 until 1943, to realize full dictatorship in Austria. Had it happened overnight, my countrymen would have fought to the last breath. Instead, we had creeping gradualism. Now, our only weapons were broom handles. The whole idea sounds almost unbelievable that the state, little by little, eroded our freedom.

After World War II, Russian troops occupied Austria. Women were raped, preteen to elderly. The press never wrote about this either. When the Soviets left in 1955, they took everything that they could, dismantling whole factories in the process. They sawed down whole orchards of fruit, and what they couldn't destroy, they burned. We called it The Burned Earth. Most of the population barricaded themselves in their houses. Women hid in their cellars for 6 weeks as the troops mobilized. Those who couldn't paid the price. There is a monument in Vienna today, dedicated to those women who were massacred by the Russians. This is an eyewitness account:

It's true . . . those of us who sailed past the Statue of Liberty came to a country of unbelievable freedom and opportunity. America is truly the greatest country in the world. Don't let your freedom slip away. After America, there isn't another place to go.

While individual experiences vary widely and this is only one individual's point of view, it is yet another warning that any time the line is crossed and nationalism is allowed to subvert God and His church, the country is in trouble and the door has been opened for every form of racism and inhumanity to thrive. At that point, we are no longer experiencing nationalism, but something else.

Real nationalism is beautiful and heroic. It is courageous and spurs countries to victory. It is triumphant, jubilant, encouraging, and unifying—the definition of patriotism.

Let us examine the familiar design as it has played out on the world's stage for several countries familiar to us all. The pattern is easy to recognize. It starts with nationalism, which in and of itself is very good. Only when it subverts God and His church does it become dangerous.

Typically, nationalism lasts for some time as the country enjoys its time of prosperity. If God is given His proper place and humility is evident, the nation will continue to thrive and be blessed by Him. But when God is pushed out of His rightful place as Creator, the pride and selfish ambition of a leader and a nation-state takes the country one step farther, inviting fascism in.

Next, in this leader's never-ending hunger for control, he welcomes fascism's twin into the picture, Marxism. Once this occurs, the nation—unless the arrogant ideology is successfully overthrown—will spiral out of control into poverty. At that point, Marxism's children, socialism and communism, easily take the throne, assuming complete control of the media and other outlets, undermining equality and every human civil right that exists. There is, however, some overlap as one part of society moves forward and another part of the nation may remain either ahead or lag behind in the process.

The progression is clear and obvious, yet we often fail to see it because of this lag.

Ideologies opposed to freedom and liberty encourage nationalism in the church but prevent the church from exercising its beliefs in the nation-state. When we see nationalism's one-sided invasion of the church, we have already lost liberty.

We can see this pattern clearly displayed in the nations of China, Russia, Cuba, Laos, Vietnam, North Korea, and Venezuela, and it is knocking on the door to take the rest of the world.

While the stage was being set for many years before with the lessening of parochialism and decentralization of government, the recordable beginning of China's fall to communism began with the Chinese Revolution of 1911.[14] Prior to this time, Imperialism and the Qing Dynasty were in need of reform. Those seeking to change imperialist rule into a constitutional monarchy had gained favorable acceptance of their demands by the Qing after a nationalist revolt in Wuchang. But before Yuan Shikai, their newly appointed leader, could take the helm, the Revolutionary Alliance under socialist leader Sun Yat-Sen, garnered the support of the southern provinces and took control of the newly formed Republic of China. The Qing then abdicated the throne in February of 1912.

The new vulnerability of the country after the First and Second World Wars, the lingering bitterness over their losses, and the lack of any organized belief in God, led China into the Chinese Revolution of 1949 immediately following World War II. This very costly civil war between the Nationalist Party and Chinese Communist Party ended on October 1, 1949, when Chinese Communist Party leader Mao Zedong declared the creation of the People's Republic of China. The nation and the world would never be the same.

After 1911, it did not take long for the leaven of communism to spread from China northward into Russia.[15] With the Bolsheviks' version of Lenin Marxism taking control after the Russian Civil War (1917–1923), racism and unimaginable crimes against humanity were unleashed. The brand of Marxism adopted by Lenin grossly miscommunicated the truths of capitalist society and promised to destroy it, and with its destruction the workers would rise. But this was a lie. The only people valued in this new government were the few high wage earners. When the few high wage earners failed to support the government and all people the government deemed peasants, the killing, torture, and racism knew no end.

In Cuba, the evolution to communism was similar, culminating with the Cuban Revolution (1953–1959). It began with an imbedded culture of corruption permeating every aspect of the government and a need for change. Prior to the revolution, a coup d'état occurred in 1952 and Fulgencio Batista, a former soldier, came to power. When Fidel Castro and a group of rebels seeking reform failed to oust Batista through the court system, they created the *26ᵗʰ of July Movement,* which didn't have much success until the group was backed financially by the Popular Socialist Party.

Cuba held a general election on November 3, 1958, electing Andrés Rivero Agüero by a 70 percent margin. Agüero's sole aim was to restore peace and a full constitutional government to Cuba. Unfortunately, Agüero was never able to take office due to the Cuban Revolution, and on January 1, 1959, Batista was out of power and Castro was in.

Many were misled by Fidel Castro, including the Catholic church. Castro, who like Hitler, was overtly ambiguous about his plans and beliefs, was a chameleon who claimed no ties to communism or socialism until he began to receive funding and support from communists in Russia and beyond. What fueled Castro was a disdain for anything with the slightest resemblance to the United States of America, and this included capitalism.

Capitalism is an economic rather than a political construct. It values individual creativity in trade, private ownership of property, and competitive free markets that serve the best interests of society, paying wages for labor. It exists for the accumulation of capital for the benefit of the society it serves.

In yet another evolution into communism, Laos was a French colony until 1953 when they found themselves caught in the middle of the Vietnam War and a power struggle between the royalists and the communists. Laos became a pawn in the power struggles of the Cold War nations who longed to influence the social and political outcomes of the nation. In the Laotian Civil War (1959–1975), the local nationals, Hmong people, were aided by the North Vietnamese army, which had a passionate stake in not wanting the American involvement to gain any victory. After the communists took control, the remaining Hmong people fought the new government and were persecuted as traitors and lackeys of the Americans. An estimated 300,000 people fled to Thailand and another approximately 40,000 died in the conflict. To this day, the people remain isolated and impoverished.[16]

Vietnam and North Korea have followed much the same pattern. We see clearly the absence of any freedoms or civil rights, widespread poverty, racism, and inhumane treatment. The communist and socialist ideologies crush any and all individualism and seek to control through fear, poverty, and torture of anyone standing in opposition.

Antithetical Race Theory rejects these forms of governing control on the basis that they stand in strict opposition to the *Holy Bible*—particularly the freedom and equality all people enjoy as children of their Creator. But while God's love is boundless, His freedom is never a license to do evil. God's intentions for the freedoms He grants us are clear:

"Live as people who are free, not using your freedom as
a cover-up for evil, but living as servants of God."

—I PETER 2:16

God has very specific guidelines for how we are to treat one another in His world. His desire for all people is that they should follow the Golden Rule: "So whatever you wish that others would do to you, do also to them, for this is the Law and the Prophets" (Matthew 7:12).

The ideologies of communism and socialism are firmly denounced throughout Scripture, and specifically in the Parable of the Pharisee and the Tax Collector.

He also told this parable to some who trusted in themselves that they were righteous, and treated others with contempt:

> Two men went up into the temple to pray, one a Pharisee and the other a tax collector. The Pharisee, standing by himself, prayed[a] thus: 'God, I thank you that I am not like other men, extortioners, unjust, adulterers, or even like this tax collector. I fast twice a week; I give tithes of all that I get.' But the tax collector, standing far off, would not even lift up his eyes to heaven, but beat his breast, saying, 'God, be merciful to me, a sinner!' I tell you, this man went down to his house justified, rather than the other. For everyone who exalts himself will be humbled, but the one who humbles himself will be exalted.

> —LUKE 18:9–14

You may ask yourself, *If this is true, why do we continue to see rampant racism in many places, and many related evils continuing?* It is because God's freedom extends to the free will of humanity. Humanity is free to follow Him. On the path that follows Him, there is equality for all men and women with no room for racism. Man is also free to reject God and follow his own path. It is along this path that we find fascism, Marxism, socialism, communism, and all forms of inequality and the devaluation of human life.

This history depicts the repeated and patterned decline of social and political regimes when failing to acknowledge the triune God and His place in the universe, while proving the blessing afforded a society acknowledging Him as its Lord.

CHAPTER 3

THE THINGS THAT DIVIDE US

"If a kingdom is divided against itself, that kingdom cannot stand. And if a house is divided against itself, that house will not be able to stand. And if Satan has risen up against himself and is divided, he cannot stand, but is coming to an end."

—MARK 3:24–26

The things that make each one of us different, distinct, and unique are not divisive in and of themselves. Think about any great partnership achieving great gains or accomplishments. If you examine the partners closely, you will find they are almost exact opposites in many ways. One is strong where the other is weak and so they complement and sharpen each other in this way, embracing these differences for their collective advantage.

When sin in our lives makes these differences seem like something other than a gift, we begin to see division and disunity rather than the complementary benefit. It can begin as simply as a misunderstanding that is handled poorly and only festers from there. Or it could be the green-eyed monster of jealousy. We've all seen this happen.

But there are some legitimate differences between us that *are* divisive and cannot be accepted, embraced, or explained away. The number one divider of people and nations is in whom or what they believe. We discussed this at length in the previous chapter and will revisit it in the chapter on culture.

If you recall the story of the Tower of Babel, the people's success was in their unity of purpose. They made great strides and progressed quickly because they were of one mind with a shared goal.

Today it is clear that agendas come in as many shapes and sizes as there are people, and this is caused by one overarching characteristic—pride. Pride has many forms. There is national pride, pride in personal accomplishments, family pride, and the list goes on and on. While many see these forms of pride as good and positive things, Antithetical Race Theory begs a differing point of view.

Researchers in the field of sociology recognize *cultural divides* as boundaries in society that separate social economic structures, opportunities for success, conventions, and styles.[17] These differences are so great that they essentially create different psychologies amongst differing cultures, hindering any type of harmonious interaction or exchange. The cultural divides then become strongholds of superiority and pride.

This is especially significant in learning to interact in international settings, as one's personal style and beliefs may create a cultural divide so great that he or she fails to even attempt to understand or try to relate to someone with such a chasm of difference.

In the historical events presented, we see demonstrated the destructive nature of pride, and Scripture supports this truth: "Pride goes before destruction, and a haughty spirit before a fall" (Proverbs 16:18).

Further, Scripture tells us to avoid those people who divide us: "I appeal to you, brothers, to watch out for those who cause divisions and create obstacles contrary to the doctrine that you have been taught; avoid them" (Romans 16:17).

While the theory does agree that the victories of a nation and personal accomplishments are to be celebrated, Antithetical Race Theory embraces humility and sees the victories of a nation, personal accomplishments, family pride, and all of these things as gifts from God, without whom they would not be possible. The Holy Bible reminds us repeatedly of this reality: "Every good gift and every perfect gift is from above, coming down from the Father of lights, with whom there is no variation or shadow due to change" (James 1:17).

We must acknowledge the Creator above the nation-state lest we follow the liberty-losing pattern of the past and find ourselves in a dire position.

What are inherent in all the things that divide us, besides pride, are selfishness and sin. Notice how James, the brother of Jesus, describes this impact:

> What is causing the quarrels and fights among you? Don't they come from the evil desires at war within you? You want what you don't have, so you scheme and kill to get it. You are jealous of what others have, but you can't get it, so you fight and wage war to take it away from them. Yet you don't have what you want because you don't ask God for it. And even when you ask, you don't get it because your motives are all wrong—you want only what will give you pleasure.
>
> —James 4:1–3

As we have seen throughout history, the creative manner in which people sin—and even more creatively *justify* their sin—knows no bounds. If we spent even half this level of creativity in the pursuit of virtue, one could only begin to imagine the wonderful world in which we would all be living now. But we will get to imagine that in a subsequent chapter.

Something deserving of a deeper dive here that divides us is chief *modis operandi* for the enemy—the imposters—who use shreds of truth wrapped in lies. The imposters are those who do Satan's bidding, sometimes unknowingly. They masquerade themselves as supporting the virtues of truth and love, but they are, in fact, supporting total opposites of these things. One would think the imposters are easily spotted, and they *are* for those trained in real virtues. But for those not trained where real truth and love are taught and modeled, the differences can be difficult to recognize.

It is much like the training of bank tellers when learning how to spot counterfeit bills. The tellers are not trained by examining counterfeit bills. The possibilities of counterfeits would be endless. They are trained by looking at real bills over and over and over again. Then when the counterfeit comes along it is patently obvious and easy to recognize. The same is true of God's truth.

So what are these counterfeit truths that divide us, and how exactly do they trick us?

The most profound counterfeit truth is that there are many paths to God. The Holy Bible tells us something clearly different: "Jesus said to him, 'I am the way, and the truth, and the life. No one comes to the Father except through me'" (John 14:6).

The devil tricks us by telling us that a loving God would never be so exclusive as to limit our path to Him. What we fail to recognize is that this one door is not exclusive. It is available to all people. There is no invitation more open than this.

Another counterfeit truth is that there is no such thing as a literal heaven and hell when Scripture tells us plainly about each. These are just a few sample passages of Scripture about each.

Revelation gives us a description of heaven:

> Then came one of the seven angels who had the seven bowls full of the seven last plagues and spoke to me, saying, "Come, I will show you the Bride, the wife of the Lamb." And he carried me away in the Spirit to a great, high mountain, and showed me the holy city Jerusalem coming down out of heaven from God, having the glory of God, its radiance like a most rare jewel, like a jasper, clear as crystal. It had a great, high wall, with twelve gates, and at the gates twelve angels, and on the gates the names of the twelve tribes of the sons of Israel were inscribed—on the east three gates, on the north three gates, on the south three gates, and on the west three gates. And the wall of the city had twelve foundations, and on them were the twelve names of the twelve apostles of the Lamb. And the one who spoke with me had a measuring rod of gold to measure the city and its gates and walls. The city lies foursquare, its length the same as its width. And he measured the city with his rod, 12,000 stadia.[d] Its length and width and height are equal.

He also measured its wall, 144 cubits[e] by human measurement, which is also an angel's measurement. The wall was built of jasper, while the city was pure gold, like clear glass. The foundations of the wall of the city were adorned with every kind of jewel. The first was jasper, the second sapphire, the third agate, the fourth emerald, the fifth onyx, the sixth carnelian, the seventh chrysolite, the eighth beryl, the ninth topaz, the tenth chrysoprase, the eleventh jacinth, the twelfth amethyst. And the twelve gates were twelve pearls, each of the gates made of a single pearl, and the street of the city was pure gold, like transparent glass. And I saw no temple in the city, for its temple is the Lord God the Almighty and the Lamb. And the city has no need of sun or moon to shine on it, for the glory of God gives it light, and its lamp is the Lamb. By its light will the nations walk, and the kings of the earth will bring their glory into it, and its gates will never be shut by day—and there will be no night there. They will bring into it the glory and the honor of the nations. But nothing unclean will ever enter it, nor anyone who does what is detestable or false, but only those who are written in the Lamb's book of life.

—Revelation 21:9–27

Scripture also warns us about hell:

> But false prophets also arose among the people, just as there will be false teachers among you, who will secretly bring in destructive heresies, even denying the Master who bought them, bringing upon themselves swift destruction. And many will follow their sensuality, and because of them the way of truth will be blasphemed. And in their greed they will exploit you with false words. Their condemnation from long ago is not idle, and their destruction is not asleep. For if God did not spare angels when they sinned, but cast them into hell[a] and committed them to chains[b] of gloomy darkness to be kept until the judgment; if he did not spare the ancient world, but preserved Noah, a herald of righteousness, with seven others, when he brought a flood upon the world of the ungodly; if by turning the cities of Sodom and Gomorrah to ashes he condemned them to extinction, making them an example of what is going to happen to the ungodly;[c] and if he rescued righteous Lot, greatly distressed by the sensual conduct of the wicked (for as that righteous man lived among them day after day, he was tormenting his righteous soul over their lawless deeds that he saw and heard); then the Lord knows how to rescue the

godly from trials,[d] and to keep the unrighteous under punishment until the day of judgment, and especially those who indulge[e] in the lust of defiling passion and despise authority.

—2 Peter 2:1–10

Nations are divided in the same way that families are divided. It is when they fail to agree about what they believe and find important—when they exchange the truth for a lie—that they will inevitably fall.

It is important to note that what we truly believe is what we actively do, not something we simply say that we believe. There is a passage in Scripture in which Jesus states this truth with much more eloquence than I can muster: "Prove by the way you live that you have repented of your sins and turned to God" (Matthew 3:8).

Doing so at a minimum gives a person the opportunity to have a legitimate divide with another claiming to follow the triune God.

CHAPTER 4

THE THINGS THAT UNITE US

"For good news came to us just as to them, but the message they heard did not benefit them, because they were not united by faith with those who listened."

—HEBREWS 4:2

I f sin, selfishness, and pride divide us, it is the opposite of these things—real virtues—that unite us. Psalm 86:11 encourages us to first unite ourselves to God when it says, "Teach me your way, O Lord, that I may walk in your truth; unite my heart to fear your name." It is only then—when we have united our hearts with His—that we can recognize and walk in real truth that has the capability of uniting us with humanity.

Psalm 133:1 tells us the obvious yet often overlooked truth, "Behold, how good and pleasant it is when brothers dwell in unity!"

But if not everyone believes real truth, how can we possibly have unity?

Ephesians 1:3–10 gives us the answer to this all-important question:

> Blessed be the God and Father of our Lord Jesus Christ, who has blessed us in Christ with every spiritual blessing in the heavenly places, even as he chose us in him before the

foundation of the world, that we should be holy and blameless before him. In love he predestined us for adoption to himself as sons through Jesus Christ, according to the purpose of his will, to the praise of his glorious grace, with which he has blessed us in the Beloved. In him we have redemption through his blood, the forgiveness of our trespasses, according to the riches of his grace, which he lavished upon us, in all wisdom and insight making known to us the mystery of his will, according to his purpose, which he set forth in Christ as a plan for the fullness of time, to unite all things in him, things in heaven and things on earth.

In an effort to create an organized civil society, there are certain desires we share. In the United States of America, these common desires are outlined in the preamble to the Constitution of the United States:

We the People of the United States, in Order to form a more perfect Union, establish Justice, insure domestic Tranquility, provide for the common defence, promote the general Welfare, and secure the Blessings of Liberty to ourselves and our Posterity, do ordain and establish this Constitution for the United States of America.[18]

The Constitution goes on to outline just exactly how these things, these common desires, might be accomplished through the government framework. But the truth is that we cannot have the kind of liberty and community that is called for here aside from the triune God. There are certain character traits called for in order to achieve this more perfect union, and they are what the Holy Bible calls the *fruit of the Spirit*. "But the fruit of the Spirit is love, joy, peace, patience, kindness, goodness, faithfulness, gentleness, self-control; against such things there is no law" (Galatians 5:22–23).

Without these character traits and without a moral framework based upon the Ten Commandments embodied in love, racism has an open invitation to thrive as James tells us: "For where jealousy and selfish ambition exist, there will be disorder and every vile practice" (James 3:16).

Every true follower of the triune God shares the belief that all people are equal in the eyes of the Creator. All have value. And all have equal worth. Galatians 3:23 tells us this when it says, "There is neither Jew nor Greek, there is neither slave nor free, there is no male and female, for you are all one in Christ Jesus."

And Philippians 2:1–14 provides a further call to unity in recognizing our equality: "So if there is any encouragement in Christ, any comfort from love, any participation in the Spirit, any affection and sympathy, complete my joy by being of the same mind, having the same love, being in full accord and of one mind. Do nothing from selfish ambition or conceit, but in humility count others more significant than yourselves. Let each of you look not only to his own interests, but also to the interests of others."

While these are the big important things that unite us, there are smaller things that unite us, too.

A smile.

A warm hug.

A wiggly puppy.

Spring rain.

Watching the beauty of the sunrise and sunset.

The song of a bird.

A silly dance.

A caterpillar along the sidewalk.

The triumph of an underdog in a race.

Holding a hand.

Sharing a favorite meal.

An inspiring word.

A real apology.

While some might find these things trite and over-simplistic, they are the things that build bridges, erase grudges, heal wounds, restore families, and even bring peace to nations. Why? Because the longing for these simple things draws us back together in humility and humanity through the One from whom they all flow—the only One who could ever fill the deepest longings within us.

CHAPTER 5

THE CONUNDRUM OF CULTURE

"Do not be conformed to this world, but be transformed by the renewal of your mind, that by testing you may discern what is the will of God, what is good and acceptable and perfect."

—ROMANS 12:2

H ave you ever watched a herd of sheep or cattle grazing on a hill? They do all right as long as the shepherd and sheepdog are around, keeping them safe from harm, rounded-up, and out of trouble. But leave them unattended for any length of time and some of them will have wandered off a cliff or into a briar patch. Others will have gotten lost and have no clue where they are or how to get back home. It almost seems as though they have a death wish when left to their own way.

Sound a bit like some people you know?

It is the same for tribes, nations, and people groups throughout history, as we have already discussed. Studies tell us that we are conditioned by the culture around us.[19] Our families, beliefs, behaviors, actions, and activities are all conditioned by the world around us. A family in which the children experience poor parenting or abuse tend to repeat the behavior in their own lives. We mimic what we see and experience. Often to be different or go against accepted practice is to be the one salmon swimming upstream. Yet we know from history that it is that one salmon that can and does make all the difference—both for good and evil. Often that upstream-swimming salmon becomes the proverbial shepherd simply because he or she wants the job and is the most persuasive in getting it.

But that is not always the case, nor is it always a good thing. More often than not we find that the one seeking power is not called or chosen by God, but rather is selfish, jealous, power-hungry, and filled with wrong motives. We know from history that wrong motives lead to devaluing human life. Devaluing human life leads to racism, oppression, slavery, abortion, human trafficking, and the list goes on.

So how do we solve this problem?

There is but one solution.

God.

A relationship with Him brings change. Someone who is not changed does not have a personal relationship with Him, for it is this change—becoming more like Him—that is the evidence of the relationship.

As stated previously, our differences in skin color have no impact on our personal worth or value. Yet the cultures of many nations—past and present—still struggle with this great truth. Even in the culture of King Solomon, whom the Holy Bible calls "wiser than all other men" (1 Kings 4:31), we find the struggle with the apparent differences in appearance.

Consider the young woman in Song of Solomon whose skin color is darker than all the rest. It is apparent from the following passage of Scripture that the dark skin of the Shulammite woman is unusual as compared with those around her, and they draw attention to this difference.

"I am very dark, but lovely, O daughters of
Jerusalem, like the tents of Kedar, like the cur-
tains of Solomon. Do not gaze at me because
I am dark, because the sun has looked upon
me. My mother's sons were angry with me;
they made me keeper of the vineyards, but my
own vineyard I have not kept!"

—Song of Solomon 1:5–6

This is one of the enigmas of culture—that we draw attention to things and people different from or unfamiliar to us. We
often simply do not know what to make of the difference. God
calls us to embrace our differences, but sin calls out many other
things. Sin can cause us to be jealous of the difference, and pride
can sometimes cause us to think less of the one who is different.
We find the same tendencies in other types of difference, as
well, far beyond skin color. These sinful tendencies often occur
simply because we are insecure—not understanding how deeply
we are loved by God—which results in us becoming fearful.

When we revisit the culture in William Wilberforce's day,
the late 1700s and early 1800s, we find that imperialism and the
slave trade were so engrained in the culture, it took a staunch
and courageous advocate to influence the House of Commons
for change. It was an uphill battle, even for someone as well-
liked and accepted as Wilberforce to influence this necessary
revolution in thinking. His dedication to the cause took some
twenty-five years of personal sacrifice and struggle.[20]

As evidenced throughout history, often the tide turning,
good or bad, can depend on the behavior of just one or two

people either doing the right or the wrong thing. It is much like someone in school speaking with a foreign accent. One student might say, "I love your accent! Where are you from?" Others hearing the comment will tend to join in with other complimentary things to say. While another person teasing, mocking, or otherwise speaking negatively about the student's accent may invite others to display bad behavior equally as easily.

Again, it is the relationship to God that makes all the difference in stemming the tide. A gang of bullies can be stopped by those courageous enough to say, "No more" in the school and take the appropriate next steps to stop the behavior. A group of oppressors in a nation can be stopped the same way.

But in schools and nations where God has been asked to leave, the basic purposes of learning, loving, nurturing, caring, growing, and discipline become much more difficult, confused, and chaotic. The *good* or civil responsibility has no foundation on which to stand. There is no Holy Bible giving structure and a framework to the system.

Consider the culture Moses dealt with as he led the Israelites from Egypt to Mount Sinai where he received the Ten Commandments, and note the racism even Moses experienced at the hands of his fellow Israelites.

"While they were at Hazeroth, Miriam and Aaron criticized Moses because he had married a Cushite woman. They said, 'Has the Lord spoken only through Moses? Hasn't he spoken through us, too?' But the Lord heard them. (Now Moses was very humble—more humble than any other person on earth.)" (Numbers 12:1–3).

Here we see that Miriam and Aaron thought less of Moses and his wife because of his wife's nationality. Clearly, they felt they were of a superior race. But God saw things differently, and the two were punished severely for unfairly judging their brother and his wife.

To take a deeper dive into the worth of a person as found in the soul and the fact that we were created in the image of a holy God, Scripture tells us this about our own creation and our value and the care extended to us: "Look at the birds of the air: they neither sow nor reap nor gather into barns, and yet your heavenly Father feeds them. Are you not of more value than they?" (Matthew 6:26)

We find throughout Scripture how valuable our lives are to God.

Luke 12:7 tells us, "And the very hairs on your head are all numbered. So don't be afraid; you are more valuable to God than a whole flock of sparrows."

John 3:16 says, "For this is how God loved the world: He gave his one and only Son, so that everyone who believes in him will not perish but have eternal life." Jesus sacrificed His own life for us because of His great love for us—the great value He places on each and every human life. We can't allow evil to twist this truth.

First Peter 2:9 defines us this way, "But you are a chosen race, a royal priesthood, a holy nation, a people for his own possession, that you may proclaim the excellencies of him who called you out of darkness into his marvelous light."

In today's culture, we find the devaluing of human life at an all-time high across the globe. Much of this is caused by the communist and other ideologies mentioned in Chapter 2 on The Human Race and Nations. These ideologies crush human creativity and denounce difference—two of the greatest things to celebrate about our humanness. This devaluation culture has led to record suicide rates around the world. Globally, suicide is the fourth leading cause of death in people between the ages of fifteen and twenty-nine.[21] It exceeds even deaths caused by automobile accidents in the United States.[22] How tragic and preventable is the fact that roughly every forty seconds, a valuable creative human life is ended.

First Corinthians 6:19–20 tells us, "Don't you realize that your body is the temple of the Holy Spirit, who lives in you and was given to you by God? You do not belong to yourself, for God bought you with a high price. So you must honor God with your body."

Exodus 20:13 commands us, "Thou shalt not kill."

Third, a *real* personal relationship with Jesus Christ fills us with peace, hope, and joy. That is a spiritual reality. It is truth. It is not dependent on circumstances or how we feel at any given moment. Trust is the foundation of any good relationship. Our relationship with Jesus Christ is the same in this respect. In order to have a real personal relationship with Him, we must trust Him and trust that He desires the very best for us in every way.

John 14:27 tells us, "I am leaving you with a gift—peace of mind and heart. And the peace I give is a gift the world cannot give. So don't be troubled or afraid."

Romans 15:13 explains the Holy Spirit's work in our lives, "I pray that God, the source of hope, will fill you completely with joy and peace because you trust in him. Then you will overflow with confident hope through the power of the Holy Spirit."

Hebrews 11:6 reminds us, "And it is impossible to please God without faith. Anyone who wants to come to him must believe that God exists and that he rewards those who sincerely seek him."

We have a real adversary, the devil. He is at the root of suicide and the darkness of depression. He takes shreds of truth and twists them and wraps them in lies.

Jesus, when talking to unbelievers in John 8:44–45, said, "For you are the children of your father the devil, and you love to do the evil things he does. He was a murderer from the beginning. He has always hated the truth, because there is no truth in him. When he lies, it is consistent with his character; for he is a liar and the father of lies. So when I tell the truth, you just naturally don't believe me!"

When God spoke to Cain in his struggle before killing his brother in Genesis 4:7, He said, "You will be accepted if you do what is right. But if you refuse to do what is right, then watch out! Sin is crouching at the door, eager to control you. But you must subdue it and be its master." If we abide in Christ, He enables us to master sin through the power of the Holy Spirit, instead of sin mastering us.

Second Timothy 1:7 gives us this promise, 'For God has not given us a spirit of fear and timidity, but of power, love, and self-discipline."

Romans 8:5–6 says it so clearly, "Those who are dominated by the sinful nature think about sinful things, but those who are controlled by the Holy Spirit think about things that please the Spirit. So letting your sinful nature control your mind leads to death. But letting the Spirit control your mind leads to life and peace."

God has a purpose for every life. The enemy would lead people to believe they have messed up to the point that their usefulness is over, but that's just another lie. As long as God has given a person breath on this earth, He has a purpose for his or her life.

Jesus tells us in John 10:10, "The thief's purpose is to steal and kill and destroy. My purpose is to give them a rich and satisfying life." And in Acts 2:28, we read, "You have made known to me the paths of life. You will fill me with joy in your presence."

The struggle, the temptation is not sin. Giving in to, dwelling on, committing the act is sin. To take a life—any life—is the ultimate act of selfishness, faithlessness, and evil. It is stepping into the shoes of God. His Word reminds us that it's not how we start, but how we finish, that matters (2 Timothy 4:7).

The devaluing of human life has become pervasive in today's culture. Beyond the crushing of creativity and exquisite differences in the manner we have been crafted by God, the current global culture, once recognizing and revering the wisdom of the aged, has devalued seniors like never before.

People aged sixty-five and older made up 16 percent of the American population in 2019. This elder population is expected to grow to 21.6 percent by 2040, and 4.9 million in this group live below the poverty line with another 2.6 million living near poverty. That is roughly 10 percent.[23]

And just how are we demonstrating a degradation of this group?

One of the most common and obvious ways we devalue seniors is in our tendency to look down on them simply because they no longer have a youthful physical appearance. This is a shocking and tragic thing to watch among many youths of today, who have not been taught to respect those older than themselves for their experience and wisdom, and for all they could learn from this amazing segment of society.

Social media has shifted the focus to self and taught an entire generation of people to value physical appearance as much greater than that which is inside and makes up the whole person. We find this evident in the demeaning manner we use to describe the aged—wrinkled, droopy, slow, not-all-there, forgetful, and helpless—to name just a few. We call them boring because they have a different way or grew up in another place and time that is different from ours.

There are doctors who now encourage euthanasia for senior citizens, advising them that their useful life is over. They tell the elderly that they are better off dead. How very tragic. No longer are they invited to live with their children, to be beloved and cared for, as our rightful sacrifice in acknowledgment of the much greater sacrifice they have made for us. Rather, we have become self-seeking without apology. We have no room in our lives for personal sacrifice and strongly defend and justify this position. We refuse to be inconvenienced in any way—even for a moment. Sadly, if we stopped long enough to listen to those voices of experience and wisdom, those younger would more than make up the time in finding their way—without stumbling—along life's path.

We have also devalued the souls of the unborn. Much like the fight against slavery in Wilberforce's day and Lincoln's day, abortion is a great evil that must be stopped. Between 2015 and 2019, there were an estimated 73 million abortions per year worldwide.[24] While abortion advocates misrepresent the issue of those opposing abortion as an assault on their reproductive rights, abortion is simply murder and has nothing to do with a woman's reproductive rights. It has everything to do with the rights of a population unable to speak for themselves. "Speak up for those who cannot speak for themselves; ensure justice for those being crushed" (Proverbs 31:8).

An unborn child should be safe and protected in the womb of the mother. This living child has value—as much value as anyone living outside the womb at any age, in any country, whether rich or poor. Notice what the Holy Bible says about the value of the unborn:

"You made all the delicate, inner parts of my body and knit me together in my mother's womb. Thank you for making me so wonderfully complex! Your workmanship is marvelous—how well I know it" (Psalm 139:13–14).

Killing is never a form of birth control and should never be considered such. How desensitized we have become that we even consider it!

And lest we regain our sensitivities as medical professionals, recently some medical schools have gone to great lengths to remove the once-familiar deterrent from both the Hippocratic Oath and the original Declaration of Geneva, penned by the World Medical Association after World War II. Note the original text of the oath taken by doctors with its specific mention of respecting human life from the time of conception:

> I solemnly pledge myself to consecrate my life to the service of humanity. I will give to my teachers the respect and gratitude which is their due; I will practice my profession with conscience and dignity; the health of my patient will be my first consideration; I will respect the secrets which are confided in me; I will maintain by all means in my power the honor and noble traditions of the medical profession; my colleagues will be my

brothers; I will not permit considerations of religion, nationality, race, party politics, or social standing to intervene between my duty and my patient; I will maintain the utmost respect for human life, from the time of conception; even under threat, I will not use my medical knowledge contrary to the laws of humanity. I make these promises solemnly, freely, and upon my honor.[25]

Contrast this with today's Hippocratic Oath, with specific reference to abortion removed:

I swear to fulfill, to the best of my ability and judgment, this covenant:

I will respect the hard-won scientific gains of those physicians in whose steps I walk, and gladly share such knowledge as is mine with those who are to follow.

I will apply, for the benefit of the sick, all measures [that] are required, avoiding those twin traps of overtreatment and therapeutic nihilism.

I will remember that there is art to medicine as well as science, and that warmth, sympathy, and understanding may outweigh the surgeon's knife or the chemist's drug.

I will not be ashamed to say, "I know not," nor will I fail to call in my colleagues when the skills of another are needed for a patient's recovery.

I will respect the privacy of my patients, for their problems are not disclosed to me that the world may know.

Most especially must I tread with care in matters of life and death. If it is given me to save a life, all thanks. But it may also be within my power to take a life; this awesome responsibility must be faced with great humbleness and awareness of my own frailty. Above all, I must not play at God.

I will remember that I do not treat a fever chart, a cancerous growth, but a sick human being, whose illness may affect the person's family and economic stability. My responsibility includes these related problems, if I am to care adequately for the sick.

I will prevent disease whenever I can, for prevention is preferable to cure.

I will remember that I remain a member of society, with special obligations to all my fellow human beings, those sound of mind and body as well as the infirm.[26]

If I do not violate this oath, may I enjoy life and art, respected while I live and remembered with affection thereafter. May I always act so as to preserve the finest traditions of my calling and may I long experience the joy of healing those who seek my help.

Even more notably absent than the specific reference to abortion in this version of the Oath is the minimal mention of God. Yet, the constraint not to play at God is a clear prohibition of abortion. And those who seek abortions are seeking help with death, not healing.

However in 2022, a group of dedicated and prestigious doctors from the United States of America drafted the following revision of the Oath, relevant to the times, but capturing the true ethical intent:

> I swear in the presence of the Almighty and before my family, my teachers and my peers that according to my ability and judgment I will keep this Oath and Stipulation:

> To reckon all who have taught me this art equally dear to me as my parents and in the same spirit and dedication to impart a knowledge of the art of medicine to others. I will continue with diligence to keep abreast of advances in medicine. I will treat without exception all who seek my ministrations, so long as the treatment of others is not compromised thereby, and I will seek the counsel of particularly skilled physicians where indicated for the benefit of my patient.

> I will follow that method of treatment which according to my ability and judgment I consider for the benefit of my patient and abstain from whatever is harmful or mischievous. I will neither prescribe nor administer a lethal dose of medicine to any patient even if asked nor counsel any such thing nor perform act or omission with direct intent deliberately to end a human life. I will maintain the utmost respect for every human life from fertilization to natural death and reject abortion that deliberately takes a unique human life.

> With purity, holiness, and beneficence I will pass my life and practice my art. Except for the prudent correction of an imminent danger, I will neither treat any

patient nor carry out any research on any human being without the valid informed consent of the subject or the appropriate legal protector thereof, understanding that research must have as its purpose the furtherance of the health of that individual. Into whatever patient setting I enter, I will go for the benefit of the sick and will abstain from every voluntary act of mischief or corruption and further from the seduction of any patient.

Whatever in connection with my professional practice or not in connection with it I may see or hear in the lives of my patients which ought not be spoken abroad I will not divulge, reckoning that all such should be kept secret.

While I continue to keep this Oath unviolated, may it be granted to me to enjoy life and the practice of the art and science of medicine with the blessing of the Almighty and respected by my peers and society, but should I trespass and violate this Oath, may the reverse be my lot.[27]

Having valuable standards enables us to value each other. When our culture tosses these things aside, it is essentially tossing aside human life. We must be courageous enough to call inhumane and devaluing actions into question and make every effort stop them.

Once we do stop them, we are not finished. Allowing a child to safely abide in and exit from the womb, we then need to value their rearing.

The Holy Bible tells us: "Train up a child in the way he should go; even when he is old he will not depart from it" (Proverbs 22:6).

The current culture no longer values the training and education of children to be the all-important and sacred task it once was. We demean the women who long to do this work as having no real or marketable skills, when what greater place could a woman possibly demonstrate these skills than in the training of her children? Home is the place in which discipline and respect must be instilled in the heart of a child with the loving hands of both mother and father united before God.

Even school teaching, once considered a calling rather than just a profession, has found itself in a much more dire place than a crossroad; it has reached a place of abandonment. Good teachers are abandoning the profession; parents are abandoning their support of good teachers; and students are no longer taught the proper respect or discipline required to succeed in the school setting or in the world.

In the United States of America, this unraveling began when God was asked to leave His position of oversight and protection in our public school systems.

Prior to 1962, it was accepted practice for schools to open with prayer and reading from the Holy Bible. In 1962, *Engel v. Vitale,* an action brought by five parents in Long Island, New York, made it unlawful to recite the Regents' Prayer, saying it constituted the establishment of state-sponsored religion and violated First Amendment rights via the Fourteenth Amendment.

In 1963, *Abington School District v. Schempp* made public school-sponsored reading of the Holy Bible and other religious activities unlawful. Yet at this time, these practices were so ingrained in our culture, there was little enforcement. We still had the Ten Commandments posted in many schools and courthouses across the country at the time.

Murray v. Corlett, also in 1963, served to make daily reading of the Holy Bible and The Lord's Prayer unlawful. This lawsuit was widely publicized as Madalyn Murray (O'Hair, nee Mays), an atheist, was very vocal in her protest. Her son, William Murray, III, later became a Christian pastor, having deep regret for his mother's actions.[28]

In 1971, *Lemon v. Kurtzman* established the Lemon Test for religious activities that could and could not be conducted in schools. Then in the early 2000s, several Texas lawsuits further served to squeeze God out of our schools. The evidence of what this has accomplished in the lives of our children is overwhelming and undeniable. It is not gun control but God whom we need in our schools.

Closely tied and further damaging our children is the devaluation of our God-given sexual orientation. In the beginning chapter of this book, it was mentioned that God's distinctions for humanity had to do with their sexual orientation, that being either male or female. In God's kingdom on earth, men and women were created differently for very specific roles, with each having equal value. Homosexuality and all of its derived forms are contrary to God's plan and have at their root some form of evil. The Holy Bible speaks explicitly about such.

> Or do you not know that the unrighteous will not inherit the kingdom of God? Do not be deceived: neither the sexually immoral, nor idolaters, nor adulterers, nor men who practice homosexuality, nor thieves, nor the greedy, nor drunkards, nor revilers, nor swindlers will inherit the kingdom of God.

—1 CORINTHIANS 6:9–10

Further, we read,

> Now we know that the law is good, if one uses it lawfully, understanding this, that the law is not laid down for the just but for the lawless and disobedient, for the ungodly and sinners, for the unholy and profane, for those who strike their fathers and mothers, for murderers, the sexually immoral, men who practice homosexuality, enslavers, liars, perjurers, and whatever else is contrary to sound[c] doctrine, in accordance with the gospel of the glory of the blessed God with which I have been entrusted.
>
> —1 Timothy 1:8–11

Minimizing God-given roles of men and women, trying to force each into society's box, and denying the inherent difference between males and females is to devalue them. This devaluation has given a green light to all sorts of evil, helping it to flourish. We must sound the alarm long and loud to save both children and adults from this great deception.

There is little wonder that so many artificial genders are being "created." It is a sad attempt to make sense of the chaos caused by our culture devaluing the role of the man and the role of the woman. Rather than embracing each other's differences, we mock them and demean them, as though some jobs and tasks are more important than others.

But sadly, it is the effort to subvert the role of God, once again, that sits at the root of this movement. The advancement of those perverting natural sexuality between man and woman and desiring to preempt God in choosing their own gender was at the beginning of this movement's recorded history. In America, the year 1924, Henry Gerber, a German immigrant and United States Army soldier in World War I, formed the Society for Human Rights in an attempt to overturn and gain acceptance for the act of sodomy, something that was thriving in small circles within his home nation of Germany.[29]

In 1950, Harry Hay founded a similar organization in Los Angeles called the Mattachine Foundation. Both Hay and his partner, Dale Jennings, were communists, with communism on a determined path to destroy the institution of family in America and the truth of the Holy Bible.

The American Psychiatric Association listed homosexuality as a mental illness in 1952.[30]

In 1955, Christine Jorgensen became the first male to undergo surgery for transitioning to a female. Christine Jorgensen was also a self-proclaimed communist.[31]

The year 1965 saw the publication of the book *Sexual Hygiene and Pathology* by Dr. John Oliven, who coined the term *transgender*.

In 1984, the human immunodeficiency virus (which causes AIDS) was spreading widely among homosexual men and was determined by the Centers for Disease Control and Prevention to be a direct result of sodomy.[32]

The Holy Bible warns us of such consequences in the book of Romans: "And the men, instead of having normal sex relationships with women, burned with lust for each other, men doing shameful things with other men and, as a result, getting paid within their own souls with the penalty they so richly deserved" (Romans 1:27).

In recent decades, anti-Christian ideologies have permeated global culture to allow for the advancement of all kinds of sexual confusion and perversion, destroying and devaluing the beautiful, healthy, and fulfilling sexual plan of our Creator.

Our global culture has also devalued the covenant of marriage and the institution of family. According to the United States Census Bureau statistics from 2022, approximately four out of every ten children were born to unwed mothers. Nearly two-thirds of these were born to women under the age of thirty. One in four children under the age of eighteen—roughly thirteen million—in 2022 were being raised in homes where there is no father. Out of about eleven million single-parent families with children under the age of eighteen, 80 percent were headed by single mothers, with more than half of these single mothers never marrying.[33]

Gone are the days when we refer to each other as husband and wife, in accordance with God's design. The common term used now is the non-gender term of *partner*, as though it were a temporary business arrangement rather than the covenant lifetime bond intended by God.

But it's not too late to return to that place. Notice what Scripture says about God's design for marriage: "Therefore a man shall leave his father and his mother and hold fast to his wife, and they shall become one flesh" (Genesis 2:24).

This design for marriage and the family is repeated throughout the Gospels (Matthew 19:5; Mark 10:7).

And notice what Scripture says about the strength of marriage, and its third cord, God:

> Two are better than one, because they have
> a good reward for their toil. For if they fall, one
> will lift up his fellow. But woe to him who is
> alone when he falls and has not another to lift

him up! Again, if two lie together, they keep
warm, but how can one keep warm alone? And
though a man might prevail against one who
is alone, two will withstand him—a threefold
cord is not quickly broken.

—ECCLESIASTES 4:9–12

Enemy ideologies recognize that the strength of a nation is
found in the strength of its families. It is only when the family
is destroyed that the nation can be conquered.

While a civil society can survive on a foundation of conscience, family, and a police presence, it will only thrive when
this conscience has an anchor. This anchor has historically
been the church. But what happens when that anchor for the
conscience becomes seared as with a hot iron and is no longer
trustworthy itself?

Now the Holy Spirit tells us clearly that in
the last times some will turn away from the
true faith; they will follow deceptive spirits
and teachings that come from demons. These
people are hypocrites and liars, and their con-
sciences are dead.

—1 TIMOTHY 4:1–2

What has happened to the church in recent years is no
different from what Martin Luther addressed in his day when
posting his ninety-five theses on the door of the church in
Wittenberg, Germany, on October 31, 1517. It is no different
from what Dietrich Bonhoeffer addressed in his book, *The Cost
of Discipleship.* Their point was that the church's own conscience

is dead. The church has sold its own soul to the devil and invited the culture in, despite the warnings from Scripture to be different.

> Do not be conformed to this world, but be transformed by the renewal of your mind, that by testing you may discern what is the will of God, what is good and acceptable and perfect.
>
> —ROMANS 12:2

When the church embraces homosexuality, its conscience is dead.

When the church allows marriage to be redefined as anything other than between one man and one woman, it has sold its soul.

When the church allows nationalism to subvert God, it is no longer true nationalism, and the church has lost its way.

When the church justifies racism and slavery, it has gone astray.

When the church fails to love *all* people, it is devoid of God.

When the church recognizes any truth other than the person of Jesus Christ as Savior for the souls of humanity, it has ceased to be His church.

I would be remiss not to mention law enforcement at this juncture, as a stable civil society embraces a police presence in the support of keeping peace for all of its citizens. The year 2013 in the United States of America saw the formation of a Marxist group called Black Lives Matter by three young women, Patrisse Cullors, Alicia Garza, and Opal Tometi. Their goal seemed innocent enough to some, promoting civil justice for those of black color and other minorities. But anytime one race has promoted itself above another, it has become racist in and of itself and precludes its own goal of humanity for all.

Clearly, this movement was not one interested in civil rights. This is a communist organization whose founders are trained in and promoting a Marxist philosophy that seeks to destroy law enforcement, family, and conscience at any cost.[34] Sadly, Americans have bought into the lie and taken the bait, hook, line, and sinker.

Following are the mission and vision of Black Lives Matter, taken from their own website:

Mission

Black Lives Matter Global Network Foundation is working inside and outside of the system to heal the past, re-imagine the present, and invest in the future of Black lives through policy change, investment in our communities, and a commitment to arts and culture.

Vision

Black Lives Matter Global Network Foundation imagines a world where Black people across the diaspora thrive, experience joy, and are not defined by their struggles. By achieving liberation, we envision a future that is fully divested from police, prisons, and all punishment paradigms to be replaced with investment into justice, joy, and culture.[35]

It is the very definition of racism to consider and elevate only one race of people over another.

While one would agree that there is need for reform in every organization—including law enforcement—this organization's goal is to abolish any and all police presence, prisons, as well as any and all punishment as deterrent to commit crime—clearly Marxist ideology.

This is undeniably a communist agenda that must be stopped if a free society is to continue.

Perhaps the greatest contributor and propagator of the communist mindset in America and around the globe is on the media and technology front. Think about how much things have changed in terms of the media's permissions and reach, and the impact this has had on culture nationally and globally—and the culture's desire for the sensational to the detriment of its children and people of every age.

Considering the movie and television industry in the United States of America, the Federal Communications Commission (FCC) began its oversight of this space in 1934, being primarily concerned with radio transmissions to a broad public audience.

In 1953, the state of Oklahoma televised the first trial— previously off-limits—of a teen who killed Trooper Johnnie Whittle in the driveway of the patrol headquarters as Whittle was taking the teen in for questioning. The FCC allowed the sensational televised trial without incident. Sensational programming brought ratings, and ratings equated to dollars. This formula continues to the present, and we continue to sell the souls of our children to the mainstream media.

In 1956, Elvis Presley appeared on the *Ed Sullivan Show*, with many concerns from mothers across the country regarding his hip gyrations. This led to his 1957 appearance on the show being censored to show him only from the waist up.

In 1977, three different television miniseries pushed the envelope in airing frontal nudity without any interference from the FCC.

This continued until *FCC v. Pacifica* in 1978 in which the Supreme Court ruled that the FCC had the authority to restrict broadcasts considered to be indecent in response to George Carlin's radio broadcast. Justice John Paul Stevens wrote the majority opinion for the court, suggesting how radio and television broadcasts differ from print media as follows:

> First, the broadcast media have established a uniquely pervasive presence in the lives of all Americans. Patently offensive, indecent material presented over the airwaves confronts the citizen, not only in public, but also in the privacy of the home, where the individual's right to be left alone plainly outweighs the First Amendment rights of an intruder. Because the broadcast audience is constantly tuning in and out, prior warnings cannot completely protect the listener or viewer from unexpected program content. To say that one may avoid further offense by turning off the radio when he hears indecent language is like saying that the remedy for an assault is to run away after the first blow. One may hang up on an indecent phone call, but that option does not give the caller a constitutional immunity or avoid a harm that has already taken place.
>
> Second, broadcasting is uniquely accessible to children, even those too young to read. Although Cohen's

written message might have been incomprehensible to a first grader, Pacifica's broadcast could have enlarged a child's vocabulary in an instant. Other forms of offensive expression may be withheld from the young without restricting the expression at its source.[36]

The current movie rating system began in 1968 when the former Hays Code's moral censorship guidelines with very specific content rules were replaced by new Motion Picture Association of America Chairman Jack Valenti. Valenti's revolutionary new guidelines, which allowed any and all movies to be shown, employed a parent-driven committee to subjectively rate and evaluate the content of movies based on what they deemed appropriate at the time. This subjective system's acceptability ratings have changed drastically over the years—allowing increased profanity, nudity, and violence to younger audiences—indicating the growing desensitization of an ever-eroding culture.

Video games and the ease with which they may be purchased have further led to the destruction of our children and families. One need only examine movies or video games now versus twenty or even ten years ago to recognize the massive shift in the desensitization of the culture and what is considered acceptable in this unique form of entertainment.

Lest we gloss over the communist ties here to the media, the communist Chinese have significant stakes in both our television news, motion picture, and video game companies, giving rise to increasingly anti-family, anti-conscience, and anti-law enforcement rhetoric.[37]

There is significant value in sharing the following transcript of Walt Disney's testimony before the House Un-American

Activities Committee in October of 1947, as it indicates the importance with which Americans recognized the infiltration of communist ideologies upon a free society's culture:

> **Investigator:** "Mr. Disney, will you state your full name and present address, please."
>
> **Disney:** "Walter E. Disney, Los Angeles, California" . . .
>
> **Investigator:** "What is your occupation?"
>
> **Disney:** "Well, I am a producer of motion picture cartoons."
>
> **Investigator:** "Where are [your] films distributed?"
>
> **Disney:** "All over the world."
>
> **Investigator:** "In all countries of the world?"
>
> **Disney:** "Well, except the Russian countries."
>
> **Investigator:** "Why aren't they distributed in Russia, Mr. Disney?"
>
> **Disney:** "Well, we can't do business with them."
>
> **Investigator:** "What do you mean by that?"
>
> **Disney:** "Well, we have sold them some films a good many years ago. They bought the *Three Little Pigs* [1933] and used it through Russia. And they looked at a lot of our pictures, and I think they ran a lot of them in Russia, but then turned them back to us and said they didn't want them, they didn't suit their purposes" . . .

Investigator: "Have you ever made any pictures in your studio that contained propaganda and that were propaganda films?"

Disney: "Well, during the war we did. We made quite a few, working with different government agencies. We did one for the Treasury on taxes and I did four anti-Hitler films. And I did one on my own for air power" . . .

Investigator: "Aside from those pictures you made during the war, have you made any other pictures, or do you permit pictures to be made at your studio containing propaganda?"

Disney: "No, we never have. During the war, we thought it was a different thing. It was the first time we ever allowed anything like that to go in the films. We watch so that nothing gets into the films that would be harmful in any way to any group or any country. We have large audiences of children and different groups, and we try to keep them as free from anything that would offend anybody as possible. We work hard to see that nothing of that sort creeps in."

Investigator: "Do you have any people in your studio at the present time that you believe are Communist or Fascist, employed there?"

Disney: "No, at the present time I feel that everybody in my studio is 100 percent American."

Investigator: "Have you had at any time, in your opinion, in the past, have you at any time in the past had any Communists employed at your studio?"

Disney: "Yes, in the past I had some people that I definitely feel were Communists."

Investigator: "As a matter of fact, Mr. Disney, you experienced a strike at your studio, did you not?"

Disney: "Yes."

Investigator: "And is it your opinion that that strike was instituted by members of the Communist Party to serve their purposes?"

Disney: "Well, it proved itself so with time, and I definitely feel it was a Communist group trying to take over my artists and they did take them over."

Investigator: "Do you say they did take them over?"

Disney: "They did take them over" . . .

Investigator: "In other words, Mr. Disney, Communists out there smeared you because you wouldn't knuckle under?"

Disney: "I wouldn't go along with their way of operating. I insisted on it going through the National Labor Relations Board. And he told me outright that he used them as it suited his purposes" . . .

Investigator: "What is your personal opinion of the Communist Party, Mr. Disney, as to whether or not it is a political party?"

Disney: "Well, I don't believe it is a political party. I believe it is an unAmerican thing. The thing that

I resent the most is that they are able to get into these unions, take them over, and represent to the world that a group of people that are in my plant, that I know are good, 100 percent Americans, are trapped by this group, and they are represented to the world as supporting all of those ideologies, and it is not so, and I feel that they really ought to be smoked out and shown up for what they are, so that all of the good, free causes in this country, all the liberalisms that really are American, can go out without the taint of communism. That is my sincere feeling on it."

Investigator: "Do you feel that there is a threat of Communism in the motion picture industry?"

Disney: "Yes, there is, and there are many reasons why they would like to take it over or get in and control it or disrupt it, but I don't think they have gotten very far, and I think the industry is made up of good Americans, just like in my plant, good, solid Americans. My boys have been fighting it longer than I have. They are trying to get out from under it and they will in time if we can just show them up."

Investigator: "There are presently pending before this committee two bills relative to outlawing the Communist Party. What thoughts have you as to whether or not those bills should be passed?"

Disney: "Well, I don't know if I qualify to speak on that. I feel if the thing can be proven un-American that it ought to be outlawed. I think in some way it should be done without interfering with the rights of the people. I think that will be done. I have that faith. Without interfering, I mean, with the good, American rights that we all have now, and we want to preserve."

Investigator: "Have you any suggestions to offer as to how the industry can be helped in fighting this menace?"

Disney: "Well, I think there is a good start toward it. I know that I have been handicapped out there in fighting it because they have been hiding behind this labor setup, they get themselves closely tied up in the labor thing, so that if you try to get rid of them they make a labor case out of it. We must keep the American labor unions clean. We have got to fight for them."

Investigator: "Mr. Disney, you are the fourth producer we have had as a witness, and each one of those four producers said, generally speaking, the same thing— and that is that the Communists have made inroads, have attempted inroads. I just want to point that out because there seems to be a very strong unanimity among the producers that have testified before us. In addition to producers, we have had actors and writers testify to the same. There is no doubt but what the movies are probably the greatest medium for entertainment in the United States and in the world. I think you, as a creator of entertainment, probably are one of the greatest examples in the profession. I want to congratulate you on the form of entertainment which you have given the American people and given the world and congratulate you for taking time out to come here and testify before this committee. He has been very helpful" . . . [38]

This interview is significant because it demonstrated a very real threat to America. It also demonstrated that Americans at the time were aware of the very real threat of communism, and they understood what it could and would do to their culture.

And now we have fallen asleep.

The cancel culture that began to take hold of the world, creating new words like *disinformation*, exploded during the COVID-19 pandemic in a clear effort to control conversations, outcomes, health care, the flow of money, statistics, and the spread of an aggregated ideology that is devoid of creative thought and the belief in a creative triune God. It is George Orwell's *Nineteen Eighty-Four* come to life.

As the motion picture, television, and video game industries as a whole have deteriorated, there are bright spots on the horizon. And lest the script become too negative, courageous men and women continue to make valuable, worthwhile television programs, movies, and video games that have a lasting positive impact on the world and our children. I applaud the work of Jon and Andrew Erwin, Stephen and Alex Kendrick, Pure Flix™, and many, many others. These companies and individuals should be encouraged and celebrated for their courage and willingness to go against the grain.

Akin to these industries and their impact on culture and racism is that of technology. In 1989, it was British nuclear researcher Tim Berns-Lee's proposal for what would become the World Wide Web that has changed the communication and culture landscape most in the past few decades. Sergey Brin and

Larry Page of Stanford University then invented the Google search engine in 1996, and the Dot-com Revolution was born, with millions of people eager to join in this new internet technology and the wealth it promised.

The introduction of the iPhone by Apple came in June of 2007, and it was intended to be a cross between the cellular phone and tablet computer. Since that time, people everywhere consider the iPhone, or any number of smartphone brands, their constant companion. They feel better off forgetting the keys to their home, rather than make it out of the home without their smartphone. But just what is this dependence doing to our culture?

While there are positive impacts, such as the ability to communicate at lightning speed with people all over the world and the ability to organize our lives like never before, it seems the negative impacts of lost creativity, wasted time, addiction, distraction, and depression far outweigh the benefits. Rather than freeing up time by making tasks easier and faster to accomplish, the average person checks their smartphone every twelve minutes—whether they need to or not—spending an average of five hours per day on the device.[39] This far surpasses any efficiencies gained in organization, convenience, productivity, or ease of communication. Not to mention the mental health consequences on all ages tending to isolate themselves with the device rather than engaging in healthy human interaction.

Of significant note is the fact that the iPhone's inventor, Steve Jobs, did not allow his children to use the iPhone or iPad, citing he did not feel the use of technology was healthy for them.[40] Very telling, indeed.

Worst of all, we devalue our neighbors, our co-workers, our own family members, and our brothers and sisters in faith. Every. Single. Day.

We devalue them when we are too busy for them and when we fail to care for them or help them, knowing they are in need. We devalue them when we put our self-interest above their need. We devalue them when we fail to share our lives with them and invite them into our homes. We devalue them when we fail to demonstrate truth and love to them.

The Holy Bible admonishes us with the following: "For you were called to freedom, brothers. Only do not use your freedom as an opportunity for the flesh, but through love serve one another" (Galatians 5:13).

And also: "So whoever knows the right thing to do and fails to do it, for him it is sin" (James 4:17).

In many—if not most—of these examples, it is money and the greed to have more of it that has led to the devaluation of human life. A culture valuing money or anything else above loving God and the people created in His image, is doomed to failure. Notice what the Holy Bible says about the matter: "No one can serve two masters, for either he will hate the one and love the other, or he will be devoted to the one and despise the other. You cannot serve God and money" (Matthew 6:24).

> For the love of money is the root of all kinds of evil. And some people, craving money, have wandered from the true faith and pierced themselves with many sorrows.
>
> —1 TIMOTHY 6:10

But understand this, that in the last days there will come times of difficulty. For people will be lovers of self, lovers of money, proud, arrogant, abusive, disobedient to their parents, ungrateful, unholy, heartless, unappeasable, slanderous, without self-control, brutal, not loving good, treacherous, reckless, swollen with conceit, lovers of pleasure rather than lovers of God, having the appearance of godliness, but denying its power. Avoid such people.

—2 TIMOTHY 3:1–4

And the Holy Bible gives us this ultimate hope, as well. "Hatred stirs up strife, but love covers all offenses."

—PROVERBS 10:12

"Above all, keep loving one another earnestly, since love covers a multitude of sins."

—1 PETER 4:8

Antithetical Race Theory asserts that we are each called to be that salmon swimming upstream in the midst of a culture's strong negative current if we are to be used by God in effecting positive and necessary change in the lives of every person we meet by loving them as He does.

I pray that we would awaken from our sleep and recognize the socialistic constraints and progressive ideologies around us.

"Wake up from your drunken stupor, as is right, and do not go on sinning. For some have no knowledge of God. I say this to your shame."

—1 CORINTHIANS 15:34

The progressive culture has even penetrated many local churches, as they have embraced these deceptions, even removing the timeless wisdom of hymns.

One hymn epitomizing the truth presented in this chapter is "Rescue the Perishing" written in 1869 by Frances J. (Fanny) Crosby. The lyrics are as follows:

Rescue the Perishing

Rescue the perishing, care for the dying,
Snatch them in pity from sin and the grave;
Weep o'er the erring one, lift up the fallen,
Tell them of Jesus, the mighty to save.

Refrain:

Rescue the perishing, care for the dying,
Jesus is merciful, Jesus will save.

Though they are slighting Him, still He is waiting,
Waiting the penitent child to receive;
Plead with them earnestly, plead with them gently;
He will forgive if they only believe.

Down in the human heart, crushed by the tempter,
Feelings lie buried that grace can restore;
Touched by a loving heart, wakened by kindness,
Chords that were broken will vibrate once more.

Rescue the perishing, duty demands it;
Strength for thy labor the Lord will provide;
Back to the narrow way patiently win them;
Tell the poor wand'rer a Savior has died.

You would be hard-pressed to hear this hymn in many of today's Christian churches. What we do find in the American church is a false gospel being peddled like never before. Churches teaching salvation by grace through faith in Jesus Christ alone are few and far between. Entertainment, psychology, and secular humanism have replaced the Holy Bible in many congregations across America and beyond.

A 2022 study conducted by the Cultural Research Center (CRC) at Arizona Christian University provides some shocking statistics with regard to the culture's influence upon the American church.

Just slightly over 37 percent of Christian pastors claim to hold a biblical worldview, with 62 percent of pastors holding a hybrid worldview known as *Syncretism*. *Syncretism* is a hodgepodge of the Holy Bible, culture, and intellectual thought. No longer do these pastors consider the Scriptures to be the ultimate authority for the life of faith.

George Barna, Director of CRC, states: "A person's worldview primarily develops before the age of 13, then goes through a period of refinement during their teens and twenties. Therefore, from a worldview development perspective, a church's most important ministers are the Children's Pastor and the Youth Pastor," Barna said.[41]

The study goes on to state that only 12 percent of children's and youth pastors hold a biblical worldview, with only 13 percent of teaching pastors holding a biblical worldview. It is proof positive that the culture is influencing the American church, rather than the church influencing the culture, and *it is the greatest of all causes for alarm.*

Antithetical Race Theory is sounding the alarm regarding the condition of the culture in America and across the globe. The evidence of a once properly-placed nationalism now subverting the place of God in our churches and our families is indicative that we have already lost liberty.

But there is hope.

If those united by their belief in the triune God will heed the call of Scripture, this liberty will be returned.

> "If my people who are called by my name humble themselves, and pray and seek my face and turn from their wicked ways, then I will hear from heaven and will forgive their sin and heal their land."
>
> —2 CHRONICLES 7:14

CHAPTER 6

THE DREAM

"Unless the Lord builds the house, those who build
it labor in vain. Unless the Lord watches over the
city, the watchman stays awake in vain."

—PSALM 127:1

The dream of Antithetical Race Theory is analogous to the
dream delivered to the people on August 28, 1963, at the
Lincoln Memorial in Washington, D.C., by Martin Luther King,
Jr. It is the same dream of the Jews and the infirm persecuted in
Nazi Germany, decried by an evil empire. Throughout history
race after race and nation after nation has allowed pride and
evil to permeate the culture, like the leaven of the Pharisees in
Jesus' day.

Is there any wonder the following words by Winston
Churchill, delivered May 9, 1946, before the States-General
in Holland after World War II, have stood the test of time—
tasting still as sweet as when first delivered to the crowd hungry
for equality, truth, a proper nationalism, peace, real democracy,
and freedom on that day in history? It is a call to unity, courage,
and very specific action like no other of its time.

> **Mr. Churchill:** Mr. Speaker, you do me great honour
> in inviting me to speak to the States-General of

Holland today. I see in all this the regard which you have for my dear country and the relief which you had especially in gaining liberty against the invader. I thank you. Personally I have always worked for the cause of liberty against tyranny and for the steady advancement of the causes of the weak and poor.

This is not, as you know, the first time I have had the opportunity of addressing august or famous Assemblies. I have already addressed the Congress of the United States, the Parliaments of Canada and Belgium, the General Assembly of Virginia and besides these there is always the House of Commons at home, where, from time to time, I venture still to speak a word or two.

Let me in my turn present you my compliments upon the progress made in this country since the expulsion of the German invaders. Holland has regained stability and strength in Europe with great rapidity. I offer my respectful congratulations to all public men who, without regard to Party or interests, have contributed to this achievement. The stability of the Constitution of the Netherlands, centering upon the union of Crown and people, is an example to many countries. I trust that your affairs abroad will prosper equally with those at home.

Holland and freedom

In Britain we know and value the services which Holland has rendered to European freedom in ancient and in recent times. The Four Freedoms which the great President Roosevelt proclaimed have always been cherished in Holland and were carried by his forebears in their blood to the New World. Even in the days of the Roman Empire. the Batavian Republic had established a unique position. In the long, fierce convulsions in Europe which followed the Reformation, Holland and England were united as the foremost champions of Freedom. In those struggles after that change in the human mind which followed the Reformation long after the collapse of the Roman Empire, Holland and England were left as the foremost upholders of freedom. Our ancestors stood together on the bloody dykes, and there are few cities in the Netherlands which do not enshrine the memories of brave resolves and famous feats of arms.

Bitter were the struggles of those old days and desperate were the odds you had to face. Looking across the generations I like to feel how Britain's stand in 1940 and 1941 resembled the glorious hour when William the Silent declared that rather than surrender, the Dutch would die on the last dyke. Holland gave us King William the Third, who led both our countries against the overweening tyranny of Louis XIV. And after him John Churchill was commander-in-chief not only of the British but of the far larger armies maintained by the Dutch Republic, when she had risen through freedom and independence to power and greatness 250 years ago.

"Liberalising forces"

Her Majesty the Queen and the Government of the Netherlands have made me a gift which will be for me forever an honour and a treasure. They have presented me with the 613 letters which John Churchill wrote to the Grand Pensionary during the long ten years of the Grand Alliance, which alliance he directed, largely formed and finally crowned with victory. I express again to this meeting of both your Houses my gratitude and that of my family for this extraordinary mark of your kindness to me.

Since the bygone struggles between Protestants and Catholics of the sixteenth and seventeenth centuries, there is at least one profound and beneficent new fact of which all should take account. The Church of Rome has ranged itself with those who defend the rights and dignity of the individual, and the cause of personal freedom throughout the world. I speak of course as one born of a Protestant and Episcopalian family, and I rejoice to see the new and ever-growing unity in lay matters, and not perhaps in lay matters only, between all the Christian churches with those liberalising forces which must ever light the onward march of man.

Holland in the Second World War

Let me pay my tribute to the part borne by Holland in the overthrow of Hitler's hideous tyranny. After your troops and water defences had been overwhelmed by the sudden, treacherous onslaught, which happened six years ago tomorrow, the Dutch people had no longer the means to maintain organised armies in the field, but the will power and firmness of character shown during the grim years of foreign oppression and occupation were definite factors in the ultimate downfall of Nazism, and the Resistance Movement, for which so many thousands of patriots gave their lives, played an even more important part.

In Britain we understand how you must have suffered in these years of torment of soul and mind to which starvation and bombardment were lesser afflictions. All honour to those who perished for the cause. May their memory cement the unity of all true Dutchmen. I thank you on behalf of Great Britain for your work. I am glad to meet here my friend, Professor Gerbrandy, the former Prime Minister, who was in Britain with us in all the dark days and who was so vigilant and faithful a champion of the rights and interests of the Netherlands.

Gladstone on nationhood

Speaking here today, where my words may carry far and wide, it is my first duty to affirm the sanctity of the rights of smaller States. In affirming these rights, I base myself upon that grand figure of Victorian Liberalism, William Gladstone. Mr. Gladstone, in his third Midlothian speech, said on 27 November 1879:

The sound and the sacred principle that Christendom is formed of a band of nations who are united to one another in the bonds of right; that they are without distinction of great and small; there is an absolute equality between them—the same sacredness defends the narrow limits of Belgium [and of course Holland] as attaches to the extended frontiers of Russia, or Germany, or France. I hold that he who by act or word brings that principle into peril or disparagement is endangering the peace and all the most fundamental interests of a Christian society.'

The duty, Mr. Speaker, of the large powers of the modern world is to see that those rights of every nation are jealously and strictly protected. The purpose of the United Nations Organisation is to give them the sanction of international law, for which Holland and Grotius are so justly famous, and also to make sure that the force of right will, in the ultimate issue, be protected by the right of force.

On nationalism

I will now, Mr. Speaker, if you will permit me, if I do not trespass too long upon your courtesy and goodwill, speak of nationalism. Is it an evil or is it a virtue?

Where nationalism means the lust for pride and power, the craze for supreme domination by weight or force; where it is the senseless urge to be the biggest in the world, it is a danger and a vice. Where it means love of country and readiness to die for country; where it means love of tradition and culture and the gradual building up across the centuries of a social entity dignified by nationhood, then it is the first of virtues.

It is indeed the foundation of a progressive and happy family of nations. Some of our shallow thinkers and false guides—and there are many today—do not distinguish between these two separate and opposing conceptions. They mix them together and use all arguments according as their fancy or their interest prompts them. They condemn nationalism as an old-world obsession and seek to reduce us all, both countries and individuals to one uniform pattern with nothing but material satisfactions as our goal.

Or again, or sometimes with almost the same breath, they pervert the noble sentiments of patriotism to the hideous, aggressive expansion of old-world imperialism, and to the obliteration by force or by wrongful teaching of all the varieties and special cultures, all those dear thoughts of home and country without which existence, however logically planned, would be dreary and barren beyond thought or imagination.

The tragedy of Europe

After the end of the great conflict from 1914 to 1918 it was hoped that the wars were over. Yet we have witnessed an even more destructive world-wide struggle. Need we have done so? I have no doubt whatever that firm guidance and united action on the part of the victorious powers could have prevented this last catastrophe. If the United States had taken an active part in the League of Nations, and if the League of Nations had been prepared to use concerted force, even had it only been European force, in order to prevent the rearmament of Germany, there was no need for further serious bloodshed. Let us, Sir, profit at least by this terrible lesson. In vain did I try to teach it before the War.

Mr. Speaker, the tragedy of Europe shocks mankind. Well, as you said in your Address, "Europe is totally ravaged." The tragedy darkens the pages of human history. It will excite the amazement and horror of future generations. Here in these beautiful, fertile and temperate lands, where so many of the noblest parent races of mankind have developed their character, their arts and their literature, we have twice in our own lifetime seen all rent asunder and torn to pieces in frightful convulsions which have left their mark in blackened devastation through the entire continent.

And had not Europe's children of earlier times come back across the Atlantic Ocean with strong and rescuing arms, all the peoples of Europe might have fallen into the long night of Nazi totalitarian despotism.

Tasks ahead

Upon Britain fell the proud but awful responsibility of keeping the Flag of Freedom flying in the old world till the forces of the new world could arrive. But now the tornado has passed away. The thunder of the cannons has ceased, the terror from the skies is over, the oppressors are cast out and broken. We may be wounded and impoverished. But we are still alive and free. The future stands before us, to make or mar.

Two supreme tasks confront us. We have to revive the prosperity of Europe; and European civilisation must rise again from the chaos and carnage into which it has been plunged; and at the same time we have to devise those measures of world security which will prevent disaster descending upon us again.

In both these tasks Holland has an important part to play. The restoration and rebuilding of Europe, both physical and moral, as you have pointed out in your Address, Mr. Speaker, is animated and guided by the kindred themes of Liberty and Democracy. These words are on every lip. They have cheered us and helped to unify us in the struggle. They inspire our rejoicings in the hour of victory. But now that the fighting is over, it is necessary to define these glorious war cries with a little more fullness and precision.

You will pardon me, I trust, if I come a little closer to the conception of free democracy based upon the people's will and expressing itself through representative assemblies under generally accepted constitutional forms.

Tests of democracy

There are certain simple, practical tests by which the virtue and reality of any political democracy may be measured. Does the Government in any country rest upon a free, constitutional basis, assuring the people the right to vote according to their will, for whatever candidates they choose? Is there the right of free expression of opinion, free support, free opposition, free advocacy and free criticism of the Government of the day?

Are there Courts of Justice free from interference by the Executive or from threats of mob violence, and free from all association with particular political parties? Will these Courts administer public and well-established laws associated in the human mind with the broad principles of fair play and justice?

Will there be fair play for the poor as well as for the rich? Will there be fair play for private persons as well as for Government officials? Will the rights of the individual, subject to his duties to the State, be maintained, asserted and exalted? In short, do the Government own the people, or do the people own the Government?

There is the test. Here are some of the more obvious tests by which the political health and soundness of any community may be ascertained.

Instrument of security

Now let us think of our other supreme task, the building of a world instrument of security, in which all peoples have a vital interest, and assuredly none more than those in these sorely-tried Low Countries, which have sometimes been called the cockpit of Europe.

The more closely the largest Powers of today are bound together in bonds of faith and friendship the more effective will be the safeguards against war and the higher the security of all other states and nations. It is evident of course that the affairs of Great Britain and the British Commonwealth and Empire, are becoming ever more closely interwoven with those of the United States, and that an underlying unity of thought and conviction increasingly pervades the English-speaking world. There can be nothing but advantage to the whole world from such a vast and benevolent synthesis.

But we also in Britain have our Twenty Years' Treaty with Soviet Russia, which in no way conflicts with other associations, but which we hope may prove one of the sure anchors of world peace. We trust that in due course the natural unity and alliance between Great Britain and France will find reaffirmation in a new instrument. We welcome every step towards strength and freedom taken by the French people. We rejoice to see France moving forward to her old place in which if there were a void, Europe would be vitally wounded. We hope that the Western democracies of Europe may draw together in ever closer amity and ever closer association. This is a matter which should be very carefully considered and if found wise should be pressed from many angles with the utmost perseverance.

Unity of purpose

Special associations within the circle of the United Nations Organisation, such as those of which I have been speaking, or like the great unity of the British Empire and Commonwealth, or like the association which prevails throughout the Americas, North and South, far from weakening the structure of the supreme body of UNO, should all be capable of being fused together in such a way as to make UNO indivisible and invincible; above all there must be tolerance, the recognition of the charm of variety, and the respect for the rights of minorities.

There was a time when the Age of Faith endeavoured to prevent the Age of Reason, and another time when the Age of Reason endeavoured to destroy the Age of Faith. Tolerance was one of the chief features of the great liberalising movements which were the glory of the latter part of the nineteenth century, by which states of society were reached where the most fervent devotion to religion subsisted side by side with the fullest exercise of free thought. We may well recur to those bygone days, from whose standards of enlightenment, compassion and hopeful progress, the terrible 20th century has fallen so far.

I say here, as I said at Brussels last year, that I see no reason why, under the guardianship of the world organisation, there should not ultimately arise the United States of Europe, both those of the East and those of the West which will unify this Continent in a manner never known since the fall of the Roman Empire, and within which all its peoples may dwell together in prosperity, in justice and in peace.[42]

As beautifully written and delivered as these words were, there are words much greater and more profound still, coming to us from Jesus Himself in the book of John, chapter seventeen. It was Jesus' prayer for us—believers both historically and those yet to come—that we might all be one just as both the Father God and Jesus the Son are one.

It is a profound prayer. Just consider it. To think that we might love each other as human beings so deeply as to mimic toward one another the relationship between God the Father and His Son Jesus Christ. It is mind-astounding. In our broken and self-centered world, it is difficult to conceive of such an idea, yet that is exactly what Jesus prays to God the Father. How much more we know that God will, indeed, one day answer His Son's prayer in John 17:1–26:

When Jesus had spoken these words, he lifted up his eyes to heaven, and said, "Father, the hour has come;

glorify your Son that the Son may glorify you, since you have given him authority over all flesh, to give eternal life to all whom you have given him. And this is eternal life, that they know you, the only true God, and Jesus Christ whom you have sent. I glorified you on earth, having accomplished the work that you gave me to do. And now, Father, glorify me in your own presence with the glory that I had with you before the world existed.

"I have manifested your name to the people whom you gave me out of the world. Yours they were, and you gave them to me, and they have kept your word. Now they know that everything that you have given me is from you. For I have given them the words that you gave me, and they have received them and have come to know in truth that I came from you; and they have believed that you sent me. I am praying for them. I am not praying for the world but for those whom you have given me, for they are yours. All mine are yours, and yours are mine, and I am glorified in them. And I am no longer in the world, but they are in the world, and I am coming to you. Holy Father, keep them in your name, which you have given me, that they may be one, even as we are one. While I was with them, I kept them in your name, which you have given me. I have guarded them, and not one of them has been lost except the son of destruction, that the Scripture might be fulfilled. But now I am coming to you, and these things I speak in the world, that they may have my joy fulfilled in themselves. I have given them your word, and the world has hated them because they are not of the world, just as I am not of the world. I do not ask that you take them out of the world, but that you keep them from the evil one. They are not of the world, just as I am not of the world. Sanctify them in the truth; your word is truth. As you sent me into the world, so I have sent them into the world. And for their sake I consecrate myself, that they also may be sanctified in truth.

"I do not ask for these only, but also for those who will believe in me through their word, that they may all be one, just as you, Father, are in me, and I in you, that they also may be in us, so that the world may believe that you have sent me. The glory that you have given me I have given to them, that they may be one even as we are one, I in them and you in me, that they may become perfectly one, so that the world may know that you sent me and loved them even as you loved me. Father, I desire that they also, whom you have given me, may be with me where I am, to see my glory that you have given me because you loved me before the foundation of the world. O righteous Father, even though the world does not know you, I know you, and these know that you have sent me. I made known to them your name, and I will continue to make it known, that the love with which you have loved me may be in them, and I in them."

In light of the Antithetical Race Theory, the United States of America, together with all mighty nations of the world, stands at a precipice and will most certainly fall with a great destruction if they do not unite and change course recognizing from whom all blessings flow. While peace is always preferred, the freedom to worship and follow the triune God is worthy of our courage and battle.

And we must consider future generations and how best to provide them with hope in putting Antithetical Race Theory into practice.

In teaching children, evidence supports providing a positive example to follow rather than the negative (Dobbs & Arnold, 2009; Matheson & Shriver, 2005).[43] Children educated using positive examples tend also to have much deeper relationships with their peers as well as much healthier, stronger, and more stable adult interactions. Yet it is the hate-filled rhetoric of Critical Race Theory that is now being taught in public schools—kindergarten through twelfth grade, colleges, universities, and even in industry, the United States military, and most police forces.

If we desire future generations to be *colorblind* with regard to race, as Antithetical Race Theory espouses, then the positive example of such unity and courage in the Person of Truth and Love must be given them—all of them.

And this radical example of equality must begin with you and me.

EPILOGUE

This book has talked a great deal about God and the importance of having a personal relationship with Him in order to effect change in a person's life and beyond. Perhaps you do not have a relationship with God and are not quite sure what that would look like or just how to go about it. Like any good relationship, seeking to follow God begins with a conversation and an understanding of our need.

With regard to our need, we know that not one of us is perfect.

"For everyone has sinned;
we all fall short of God's glorious standard."

—ROMANS 3:23

"No one is righteous—not even one."

—ROMANS 3:10

We also recognize that sin has a consequence, and that consequence is death.

"When Adam sinned, sin entered the world.
Adam's sin brought death, so death spread to
everyone, for everyone sinned."

—ROMANS 5:12

But there is hope because of God's great love for us.

> "For the wages of sin is death, but the free gift
> of God is eternal life through Christ Jesus our
> Lord."
>
> —ROMANS 6:23

> "But God showed his great love for us by
> sending Christ to die for us while we were still
> sinners."
>
> —ROMANS 5:8

And this is how our lives are transformed:

> "If you openly declare that Jesus is Lord and
> believe in your heart that God raised him
> from the dead, you will be saved. For it is by
> believing in your heart that you are made right
> with God, and it is by openly declaring your
> faith that you are saved."
>
> —ROMANS 10:9–10

There is no way that any of us could ever be good enough to earn our salvation.

There is a story in the Holy Bible about a man named Nicodemus (John 2:23–3:21) who came to speak with Jesus at night. It was clear to Nicodemus that Jesus had been sent by God, but the concept of being *born again* was puzzling to him. Jesus explained that we must be born of water—the physical birth, and that we must also be born of the Spirit if we want to see the kingdom of God. But Nicodemus didn't understand what it actually meant to be born of the Spirit. What does that look like?

Jesus explained that being born of the Spirit is something that cannot be explained in human terms, but that by faith we simply believe.

Think about a young child before he or she has been tainted or corrupted by the world. Children trust. They believe! God wants us to believe in Him the same way that a little child does.

Matthew 18:3 tells us, "Then he said, 'I tell you the truth, unless you turn from your sins and become like little children, you will never get into the Kingdom of Heaven.'" It is this simple, childlike faith we must possess in order to please God.

The experience of how someone becomes a Christian varies widely between individuals, but according to Scripture, every salvation experience includes the following parts, though you may know them by different names:

> Believe – We must believe that Jesus Christ is God's Son, that He lived a perfect, sinless life, that He died on the cross for our sins, and was resurrected from the dead (Romans 10:9–10).
>
> Receive – We receive His gift of salvation (Romans 4:16).
>
> Repent – We must repent of our sin and turn to God (Luke 13:3, 5). Repentance is leaving our old sinful life behind and turning to follow the way of Jesus.
>
> Share – We must openly declare our faith in Jesus Christ with others (Mark 8:38; Romans 10:9–10). We can't hide Him or be ashamed of Him, though many are persecuted and killed for their belief in Him.

Baptism occurs after salvation as a demonstration to the watching world that we have repented of our sin and turned to God. It neither determines nor precludes our salvation but is an act of obedience to God.

In the Holy Bible, the act of baptism was first introduced by John the Baptist who came preparing the way for Jesus Christ. The word *baptism* or *baptize* is the transliteration of the Greek word *baptizo*, meaning "to immerse."

Jesus was baptized by John the Baptist, which brought great pleasure to the Father. Matthew 3:16–17 recounts, "As soon as Jesus was baptized, he went up out of the water. At that moment heaven was opened, and he saw the Spirit of God descending like a dove and alighting on him. And a voice from heaven said, 'This is my Son, whom I love; with him I am well pleased.'"

But why must I do all of these things when some passages of Scripture tell me I need only to believe (Acts 16:31; Ephesians 2:8)? These things are a demonstration of the act of believing. Salvation comes by God's grace through faith in Jesus Christ alone. It is not determined by our works or our merit in any way.

When we begin a personal relationship with Jesus, a change takes place. We are forgiven and free. God gives us a new heart of flesh to replace our stony, stubborn heart, and a transformation begins to take place within us. The Holy Bible tells us in 2 Corinthians 5:17 that when we become followers of Jesus, we become new persons. Our old lives are gone, and our new lives have begun!

How beautiful it is to have a new life, regardless of our age or any past sin we have ever committed. We are forgiven and free!

If you would like more information on what it means to live the Christian life on a daily basis, following are some helpful resources:

www.billygraham.org
www.peacewithgod.net
www.biblegateway.com
www.bibleproject.com

"But when the goodness and loving kindness of God our Savior appeared, He saved us, not because of works done by us in righteousness, but according to His own mercy, by the washing of regeneration and renewal of the Holy Spirit, whom He poured out on us richly through Jesus Christ our Savior, so that being justified by His grace we might become heirs according to the hope of eternal life."

—TITUS 3:4–7

ABOUT THE AUTHOR

PRISCILLA DOREMUS

A uthor Priscilla Doremus accepted Christ at the age of five and has written books, poems, and stories from a very early age. She is the author of *Prayers for Times of Crisis* and has a passion for sharing Christ through the written word.

Priscilla attended Baylor University, and has worked in the field of Insurance and Risk Management for many years. She has two children, and her family currently makes their home in Sugar Land, Texas.

For more information, visit Priscilla's blog at:

www.priscilladoremus.com

CITATIONS

[1]United States Holocaust Memorial Museum. "Introduction to the Holocaust." *Holocaust Encyclopedia*. https://encyclopedia.ushmm.org/content/en/article/introduction-to-the-holocaust. Accessed 20 May 2023.

[2]Brown, Mark. "World's Oldest Family Tree Revealed in 5,700-Year-Old Cotswolds Tomb." *The Guardian*, 22 Dec. 2021, www.theguardian.com/science/2021/dec/22/worlds-oldest-family-tree-costwolds-tomb-hazleton-north-long-cairn-dna. Accessed 20 May 2023.

[3]Johnson, Caleb. "The Mayflower Compact." *Caleb Johnson's Mayflower History*, mayflowerhistory.com/ mayflower-compact. Accessed 20 May 2023.

[4]"The First Great Awakening." *Independence Hall Association*. https://www.ushistory.org/declaration/lessonplan/ firstgreatawakening.html#:~:text=The%20First%20Great%20Awakening%20was,and%20Germany%20at%20that%20time. Accessed 20 May 2023.

[5]Hassler, Warren W. and Weber, Jennifer L.. "American Civil War." *Encyclopedia Britannica*, 11 May 2023, https://www.britannica.com/event/American-Civil-War. Accessed 23 May 2023.

[6]Lincoln, Abraham, "Transcript of the Proclamation." *National Archives*, January 1, 1863, https://www.archives.gov/exhibits/featured-documents/emancipation-proclamation/transcript.html. Accessed 20 May 2023.

[7]History.com Editors. "World War I." *History*, April 18, 2023, https://www.history.com/topics/world-war-i/world-war-i-history. Accessed 20 May 2023.

[8]Library of Congress. "The Great Depression." *Library of Congress*, https://www.loc.gov/classroom-materials/united-states-history-primary-source-timeline/great-depression-and-world-war-ii-1929–1945/world-war-ii/. Accessed 20 May 2023.

[9]The Holocaust. "The Human Toll." *Sydney Jewish Museum*, 2018, https://www.holocaust.com.au/the-facts/the-human-toll/. Accessed 20 May 2023.

[10]Wikipedia contributors. "Gulag." *Wikipedia, The Free Encyclopedia*. Wikipedia, The Free Encyclopedia, 22 May. 2023. https://en.wikipedia.org/wiki/Gulag. 20 May 2023.

[11] Biyun, Eddie. "A Time for Justice." *Talbot Magazine, Biola University*, June 16, 2021, https://www.biola.edu/blogs/talbot-magazine/2020/the-jesus-people-movement-50-plus-years-later%20imperial%20system. Accessed 20 May 2023.

[12] BGEA Admin. "From a 'Lost Hippie' to a 'Rebel': 10 Lives Touched by Billy Graham." *Billy Graham Evangelistic Association, June 20, 2018*, https://billygraham.org/story/a-lost-hippie-a-rebel-an-unsaved-brat-10-comments-from-people-whose-lives-were-touched-by-billy-graham/. Accessed 20 May 2023.

[13] Uncategorized. "Billy Graham's Life & Ministry By the Numbers." *Lifeway Research, February 21, 2018*, https://research.lifeway.com/2018/02/21/billy-grahams-life-ministry-by-the-numbers/. Accessed 20 May 2023.

[14] Office of the Historian. "The Philippine-American War, 1899–1902." *Milestones in the History of U.S. Foreign Relations*, https://history.state.gov/milestones/1899–1913/chinese-rev#:~:text=In%20October%20of%201911%2C%20a,and%20ending%20the. Accessed 20 May 2023.

[15] Wikipedia contributors. "Soviet Union." *Wikipedia, The Free Encyclopedia.* May 28, 2023, 22:50 UTC. https://en.wikipedia.org/w/index.php?title=Soviet_Union&oldid=1157483300. Accessed 20 May 2023.

[16] Gerin, Roseanne. "Impoverished Laos has lost more than $760 million to corruption since 2016: report." *Radio Free Asia, April 18, 2022*, https://www.rfa.org/english/news/laos/corruption-losses-04182022171408.html. Accessed 20 May 2023.

[17] Prentice, Deborah A., ed (2001). Cultural divides : understanding and overcoming group conflict. New York: Russell Sage Foundation. pp. 230. ISBN 0871546892.

[18] National Archives. "The Constitution of the United States: A Transcription." *The U.S. National Archives and Records Administration*, https://www.archives.gov/founding-docs/constitution-transcript. Accessed 20 May 2023.

[19] Wilson, Victoria. "Cultural Conditioning: How the World Influences Our Beliefs and Behavior." *Exceptional Futures*, https://www.exceptionalfutures.com/cultural-conditioning/#:~:text=What%20is%20Cultural%20Conditioning%3F,believe%20to%20be%20acceptable%20behaviors. Accessed 20 May 2023.

[20] The Editors of Encyclopedia Britannica. "William Wilberforce: British Politician, *Britannica*, May 3, 2023, https://www.britannica.com/biography/William-Wilberforce. Accessed 20 May 2023.

[21] World Health Organization. Suicide: key facts. Geneva: World Health Organization; 2021 [cited 2021 July 20]. Available from: https://www.who.int/news-room/fact-sheets/detail/suicide. Accessed 20 May 2023.

[22]Saunders, Heather and Panchal, Nirmita. "A Look at Suicide Rates Ahead of 988 Launch—A National Three-Digit Suicide Prevention Hotline." *KFF: The Independent Source for Health Policy Research, Polling, and News*, June 22, 2022, https://www.kff.org/other/issue-brief/a-look-a-suicide-rates-ahead-of-988-launch-a-national-three-digit-suicide-prevention-hotline/#:~:text=Nearly%20half%20a%20million%20lives,caused%20by%20motor%20vehicle%20accidents. Accessed 20 May 2023.

[23]Kochanek KD, Xu J, Arias E. Mortality in the United States, 2019. NCHS Data Brief. 2020 Dec;(395):1–8. PMID: 33395387.

[24]Guttmacher Institute. "Unintended Pregnancy and Abortion Worldwide." *Guttmacher Institute*, March 2022, https://www.guttmacher.org/fact-sheet/induced-abortion-worldwide. Accessed 20 May 2023.

[25]Editor Life Issues Institute. "Hippocratic Oath and Declaration of Geneva." *Life Issues Institute*, https://lifeissues.org/1996/06/hippocratic-oath-and-declaration-of-geneva/. Accessed 20 May 2023.

[26]Wikipedia contributors. Hippocratic Oath. Wikipedia, The Free Encyclopedia. April 16, 2023, 17:32 UTC. Available at: https://en.wikipedia.org/w/index.php?title=Hippocratic_Oath&oldid=1150165883. Accessed 20 May 2023.

[27]Editor Life Issues Institute. "Hippocratic Oath and Declaration of Geneva." *Life Issues Institute*, https://lifeissues.org/1996/06/hippocratic-oath-and-declaration-of-geneva/. Accessed 20 May 2023.

[28]Armstrong, Kayla. "Son of America's most famous atheist became a pastor." *God Reports*, April 12, 2017, https://www.godreports.com/2017/04/son-of-americas-most-famous-atheist-became-a-pastor-recounts-his-mothers-grisly-demise/. Accessed 20 May 2023.

[29]History.com Editors. "Gay Rights." *History*, April 27, 2023, https://www.history.com/topics/gay-rights/history-of-gay-rights. Accessed 20 May 2023.

[30]History.com Editors. "Gay Rights." *History*, April 27, 2023, https://www.history.com/topics/gay-rights/history-of-gay-rights. Accessed 20 May 2023.

[31]Giles-Peterson, Jules. "Communist Christine Jorgensen and the MILFs." *Sad Brown Girl*, February 12, 2021, https://sadbrowngirl.substack.com/p/communist-christine-jorgensen-and. Accessed 20 May 2023.

[32]History.com Editors. "Gay Rights." *History*, April 27, 2023, https://www.history.com/topics/gay-rights/history-of-gay-rights. Accessed 20 May 2023.

[33]SMG. "Single Mother Statistics." *SMG*, February 2, 2023, https://singlemotherguide.com/single-mother-statistics/#:~:text=According%20

Radical Equality

Radical Equality

to%202022%20U.S.%20Census,were%20headed%20by%20single%20mothers.&text=Of%20all%20single%2Dparent%-20families,were%20born%20to%20unwed%20mothers. Accessed 20 May 2023.

[34]Gonzalez, Mike. "Marxism Underpins Black Lives Matter Agenda." *The Heritage Foundation*, September 8, 2021, https://www.heritage.org/progressivism/commentary/marxism-underpins-black-lives-matter-agenda. Accessed 20 May 2023.

[35]Black Lives Matter. "Mission." *Black Lives Matter,* https://blacklivesmatter.com/transparency/#mission. Accessed 20 May 2023.

[36]Head, Tom. "History of Television Censorship." *ThoughtCo.*, February 13, 2019, https://www.thoughtco.com/ history-of-television-censorship-721229. Accessed 20 May 2023.

[37]Reuters Staff. "Fact check: DreamWorks Animation, CBS, CNBC and ABC are owned by American companies." *Reuters*, March 1, 2021, https://www.reuters.com/article/uk-factcheck-dreamworks-china/fact-check-dreamworks-animation-cbs-cnbc-and-abc-are-owned-by-american-companies-idUSKCN2AT2VM. Accessed 20 May 2023.

[38]Alpha History. "WALT DISNEY TESTIFIES BEFORE HUAC (1947)." *Alpha History,* https://alphahistory.com/ coldwar/walt-disney-testifies-huac-1947/. Accessed 20 May 2023.

[39]Yasin, Sarah. "Positive Effects Of Mobile Phone Use In Our Society And Environment." *Electronics Lovers,* April 26, 2018, https://electronicslovers.com/2018/04/the-impact-of-mobile-devices-on-our-lives-society-and-environment.html#:~:text=Nowadays%20mobile%20phones%20have%20the,to%20our%20loved%20ones%20 daily. Accessed 20 May 2023.

[40]Otero del Rio, Mariel. "Why didn't Steve Jobs let his kids use iPads?" *Houston Chronicle*, September 18, 2021,

https://www.chron.com/business/article/Why-didn-t-Steve-Jobs-let-his-kids-use-iPads-16468409.php#:~:text=Steve%20Jobs%20thought%20it%20was,of%20the%20founder%20of%20Apple. Accessed 20 May 2023.

[41]Munsil, Tracy. "New Study Shows Shocking Lack of Biblical Worldview Among American Pastors," *American Worldview Inventory CRC*, May 12, 2022, https://www.arizonachristian.edu/2022/05/12/shocking-lack-of-biblical-worldview-among-american-pastors/. Accessed 20 May 2023.

[42]Reprinted from Martin Gilbert and Larry P. Arnn, eds., *The Churchill Documents, vol. 22, Leader of the Opposition,* August 1945-September 1951 (Hillsdale College Press, 2019). Accessed 20 May 2023.

[43]Pankonin, Ashlie and Myers, Rebekah. "TEACHERS' USE OF POSITIVE AND NEGATIVE FEEDBACK: IMPLICATIONS FOR STUDENT BEHAVIOR." *Applied Psychology Opus*, Spring 2017, https://wp.nyu.edu/steinhardt-appsych_opus/teachers-use-of-positive-and-negative-feedback-implications-for-student-behavior/. Accessed 20 May 2023.

www.ingramcontent.com/pod-product-compliance
Lightning Source LLC
Chambersburg PA
CBHW022100020426
42335CB00012B/769